Wicked
LEXINGTON,
KENTUCKY

Wicked
LEXINGTON,
KENTUCKY

FIONA YOUNG-BROWN

Charleston · London

THE
History
PRESS

Published by The History Press
Charleston, SC 29403
www.historypress.net

Copyright © 2011 by Fiona Young-Brown
All rights reserved

First published 2011

Manufactured in the United States

ISBN 978.1.60949.133.8

1. Crime--Kentucky--Lexington--History--Anecdotes. 2. Violence--Kentucky--Lexington-
-History--Anecdotes. 3. Corruption--Kentucky--Lexington--History--Anecdotes. 4.
Scandals--Kentucky--Lexington--History--Anecdotes. 5. Lexington (Ky.)--Moral conditions-
-Anecdotes. 6. Lexington (Ky.)--Social conditions--Anecdotes. 7. Lexington (Ky.)--
Biography--Anecdotes. I. Title.
HV6795.L48Y68 2011
364.109769'47--dc23
2011019690

CONTENTS

Acknowledgements   7

Introduction   9

Chapter 1. Dastardly Duels   15

Chapter 2. The Lion and the Compromiser: Dueling Clays   29

Chapter 3. Wicked Women   39

Chapter 4. The Cheating Congressman   63

Chapter 5. To Be Black in Lexington   79

Chapter 6. Troubles at Transy   99

Chapter 7. Wicked Sports   107

Bibliography   119

About the Author   127

ACKNOWLEDGEMENTS

I would like to thank several people for their help in putting together *Wicked Lexington*, especially Will McKay at The History Press, Amanda Hervey and Sarah Katzenmaier. Thanks also to Eric Brooks and the staffs at the Lexington Public Library, the University of Louisville Law Library and the University of Kentucky Archives. As always, I am grateful to my husband, Nic Brown, for his continuing support and his willingness to read drafts.

Perhaps most importantly, I am forever grateful to my grandmother, Florence Curtis, for instilling in me at a young age a love of gossip about all things wicked. Rest in peace.

INTRODUCTION

The people of Lexington have long prided themselves on their city, and for good reason. They are fortunate to live in the heart of horse country, in a college town that has produced major statesmen, a First Lady, Civil War heroes, Nobel Prize winners, artists and many more notable residents. As one drives through the gently rolling fields of the horse farms, past the historic houses of a genteel past and into the downtown area, one cannot help but sense a certain amount of southern charm. But does something else lie beneath that proper exterior? Something wicked perhaps?

For the first half of the nineteenth century, Lexington was a city ahead of its time, a leader in the fledgling push for westward expansion. In 1779, a party of twenty-five men built a fort at Town Branch, what is now the corner of Main Street and Mill Street. Twelve men and one woman remained in the fort, a small affair of four cabins. At night, they could hear local Indians outside. The following year, despite a brutal winter that left food scarce and many animals dead, Fayette County came into being, and the pioneers and founding fathers of Kentucky's commonwealth trickled into the new wilderness. Among the first settlers of the town were Levi Todd, whose granddaughter, Mary, would one day become First Lady of America, and Colonel Robert Patterson, who would later head north to be one of the founders of Cincinnati. Growth of the fledgling city was slow at first—Indians, climate and the difficulty of clearing the land were all contributing factors. Merchants began to open shop in 1784, and settlers

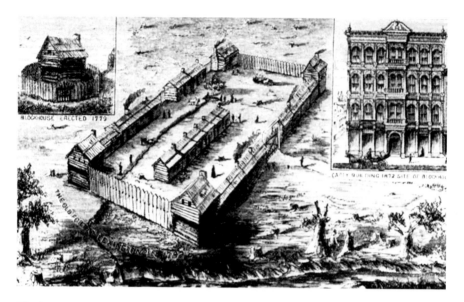

The fort at Town Branch in 1792—the beginnings of Lexington. *Courtesy of Lexington History Museum.*

established farms in the outlying areas. Hemp and tobacco were grown, and whiskey was distilled.

Perhaps there was already a hint of wickedness as far back as 1780—that is when the first jail was built. Within ten years, the need for a holding place had outgrown the small wooden hut, and a stone building replaced it. This, in turn, was replaced by a larger jail in 1819. The earliest crimes were what one might expect of any frontier town: gambling and brawling—although the brawling would not resemble any drunken fight we might happen upon today. Kentucky wrestling incorporated the use of knives and a range of techniques designed to maim the opponent: eye gouging, ear biting and testicle wrenching! Foreign visitors to the region were horrified by the level of everyday violence they encountered. Life on the frontier was rough, and the people who settled it displayed a degree of toughness that shocked a more genteel world.

One only has to recall the story of the town's first schoolmaster as an example of the ruggedness required in those early days. John McKinney began teaching lessons to the pioneer children in 1783 in a small log schoolhouse. One morning, a wildcat leapt through the schoolhouse door and onto the unsuspecting teacher. With its fangs dug into his ribs, McKinney found that no help was coming and so did what anyone would do in such a situation—he proceeded to strangle the cat to death and then removed the fangs from his bleeding torso. (Although, one could argue that a tougher man might not have canceled school for the day). This was a land where even the teachers had to be ready for anything. But in time, as Lexington expanded, the frontier moved toward the horizon. The city took on that veneer of polite society, and brawling evolved into the more gentlemanly art of dueling.

Churches formed, as did a newspaper in 1787. Although the Town Branch often flooded, spilling over its banks into the center of the town, the residents looked past such inconveniences and forged ahead. Then, in 1793, Transylvania Seminary decided to relocate permanently to Lexington. A few years later, it adopted university status. The presence of what would be one of the finest universities in the nation in the nineteenth century was a boon to Lexington and helped put it on the path to being an educational and cultural capital. With the later establishment of medical and law schools at Transylvania, Lexington went from being a small fort with thirteen occupants to the "Athens of the West," a booming center of expansion with seven thousand residents by 1833.

Lexington quickly established itself as a center of commerce. Wool factories and paper mills were constructed on what is now Manchester Street. Traders set up shop. The town prospered. Yet things did not always progress smoothly. James Prentiss, who came to Lexington in 1805 from New England to establish the paper mills, fled the town in disgrace in 1817, guilty of fraud and facing financial ruin. A Yale-educated Bostonite by the name of J.B. Borland found life in Kentucky too depressing, and in 1815 he slit his throat and jumped to his death. Such events were part of life anywhere, and Lexington was no exception. Entrepreneurs such as John Wesley Hunt helped the city to grow, both economically and politically. A number of prominent families contributed to the development of banks, business and more. Many of these names are noted around Lexington today: Hunt, Gratz, Breckinridge and Clay.

By the 1830s, Lexington not only had a university, it also had a railroad, fire stations, hotels and a state-of-the-art mental institution, one of only two in the nation. An orphanage was opened after the cholera epidemic of 1833, and the first city school was opened in 1834, offering education to the poor.

The Phoenix Hotel was the site for duels, fistfights and other colorful events in Lexington's history. It was an army headquarters during the Civil War. *Courtesy of Lexington History Museum.*

Agriculture thrived in the areas around Lexington. In addition to hemp, tobacco and corn, livestock was profitable. The city's wealthier residents built large mansions outside the town limits. Lexington was booming, but change was not far off.

Some of the very first pioneers into Kentucky were slaves. Daniel Boone's party that was attacked by Shawnees in 1775 included them, and settlers who came from Virginia brought their property, including slaves, with them when they crossed the Cumberland Gap. By the time of the Civil War, roughly one-third of the city's population was black. Lexington had become a hub for slave trading, the second-largest market in the South after New Orleans. Any black person found walking the streets alone without proper papers was liable to find himself hurled into a slave jail, to be sold down the river. There was also a strong antislavery faction within Fayette County, of which Cassius Clay was a vocal, and on occasion violent, supporter.

When war broke out in 1861, Kentuckians were torn. Although proslavery for the most part, they were also largely pro-Union, hence their status as a border state. Some historians have suggested that as the war dragged on, many in the state leaned more toward the South. It is worth noting that Kentucky was one of two states to vote for General McClellan rather than Abraham Lincoln in the 1864 election. Kentuckians were nothing if not independent, and they began to question state versus federal rights. Lexington was in the middle of the divide. Families were split. While Union forces occupied buildings on one side of Gratz Park, Confederates occupied those on the other side.

At war's end, Kentucky refused to ratify the Thirteenth Amendment ending slavery. In doing so, it became the one border state to plant itself firmly in the South, a move that caused it to experience many problems during Reconstruction—resistance to giving legal rights to freed blacks and economic difficulties associated with the end of slavery.

Notwithstanding these obstacles, Lexington managed to thrive, and as it did, the city worked hard to create an image that was both sophisticated and cultured but still very much Kentuckian. Contrary to popular belief, and despite the city's best efforts to maintain its genteel image, Lexington's history has not been as clean as many would have liked. Barely one hundred years ago, Lexington was considered one of the most wicked towns in the nation. The Athens of the West was denounced as a modern-day Sodom and Gomorrah. At the time, the blame was directed firmly toward a group of working women. Local directories show an inordinately large number of seamstresses and dressmakers, even for a city of under forty thousand. But suspicious few of these ladies spent their time huddled over a lamp with a needle in hand. Their evening activities were of a more profitable (and less moral) persuasion. Levels of vice and prostitution were such that in 1900, New York magistrate Duehl referred to Lexington as "a city of extreme wickedness." Incidentally, if you are wondering why so many chose to give their profession as seamstress, it was one of the few legitimate ways a single woman could support herself.

If you are thinking that an evening's entertainment at a typical Lexington brothel was below the cream of society, think again. As we shall see, one Lexington madam in particular made a great fortune and achieved national renown through her bordello, which attracted some of the foremost political and business figures of the region. So deep did her connections run that, in spite of being the most indicted person in the city's history, she spent not one night in jail. She has become something of a popular novelty over the decades, celebrated each year with (appropriately enough) a bed race through the heart of the city, dedicated in her honor.

Yet for all of the focus on vice and sins of the flesh as an explanation for Lexington's wicked past, politics, race and business all played equal parts. Many times, the fine gentlemen of the Bluegrass were anything but.

Wicked Lexington will explore the colorful, the scandalous and the lurid stories of this city's past—a time when political opponents fought duels in the streets, lynch mobs tried to fight their way past troops so that they could administer their own form of justice and illegal booze and women flowed freely.

Ladies and gentlemen, welcome to wicked Lexington.

Chapter 1

DASTARDLY DUELS

The people of Kentucky have a long legacy of violence. Ever since Daniel Boone followed in the footsteps of Dr. Thomas Walker, leading pioneers across the Cumberland Gap into what would become the commonwealth of Kentucky, the people who populated the state possessed a warrior mentality. They saw violence on a daily basis as they struggled to survive in the wilderness. In time, those violent tendencies developed into a sort of honor code. The feuds for which Appalachia would become known were often based on a sense of honor. Despite the popular claim that the Hatfield and McCoy feud began with a quarrel over a stolen pig, larger issues of wealth, political connections, land ownership and mineral rights played an important role in building tensions between the two families. Similarly, the French and Eversole War developed from a dispute over business contracts and land rights into a more personal conflict. Violence erupted in the streets, all in the name of honor. To quote historian Robert Ireland, "While nineteenth century Kentucky produced fine horses, hemp, and whiskey, she excelled most in crime."

Fighting on the frontier of the mountains of Appalachia could be a terrifying sight for visitors to the region. It took on a dimension of violence unknown elsewhere. Once liquor flowed, it might take little more than a look between men and knives were drawn. Historian Douglas Wilson remarked that it was "almost without rules and featured eye gouging and ear biting as regular and expected tactics." Regular fighters filed their fingernails to sharp points and oiled them before bouts; some also filed their teeth to make biting of limbs all the easier. Some visitors remarked how common it was to find backwoods men with one eye, or even with the ear or finger of another man worn proudly around their necks, souvenirs of past victories.

One should not be lulled into thinking that the violence and protection of one's name was restricted to the mountain areas of the state. Similar brawls were common in the taverns of downtown Lexington during those early decades. Far from attempting to break up such encounters, onlookers typically cheered them on eagerly, placing bets on who would be the victor. One's social status did not serve to stop the likelihood of fighting; it simply dictated where and under what conditions one might challenge an opponent. Both country and city men habitually carried on their person a dirk, or large dagger. Personal honor and the defense of it was equally important to the educated gentlemen of Lexington and elsewhere, but they would not resort to biting on the dusty floor of a local tavern; they preferred knives or guns and a more sophisticated setting. All the same, it often resulted in violence and death.

THE CODE DUELLO

The Code Duello was the name given to a series of rules regarding the protection of one's honor, drawn up by the gentlemen of Ireland in 1777. In many ways, it was similar to the codes of conduct followed by knights of old. Medieval knights had developed a romantic, idealized image, and wealthy men who now made their fortunes in business liked to imagine themselves as following in their stead. The same set of rules was followed, with some deviation, throughout Europe and America. For the well-to-do of Kentucky, it became particularly important as dueling developed from little more than a street brawl into a highly ritualized practice.

According to the Code Duello, a gentleman could hardly be expected to accept an insult or slight to the honor of himself, his family and, in some cases, even his friends. The initial offender must be given the opportunity to make a public apology. Failure to do so would mean a duel must be fought, according to terms agreed to by both parties—choice of weapons, number of shots and so on. Refusing to challenge the issuer of such a slight would result in being labeled a coward and might lead to a man's social downfall. A man might be "posted"—handbills branding him a liar and a coward would be distributed around town for all to see. The sad case of Richard Reid, a Mount Sterling judge who refused to duel, illustrates the social pressure on men to fight back in defense of honor.

Judge Reid was a man devoted to his love of three things: God, his family and the law. By 1884, he had served on the Kentucky Superior Court for two years and had gained a reputation as a wise, capable judge. A vacancy arose on the court of appeals, and so he entered the race for that seat, with many believing that he would win. As one might expect with a career in the legal profession, his decisions did not always please everyone. John Jay Cornelison, another local attorney, felt that Reid had discredited him in a case and invited the judge to his office, where he set to beating him with his cane. Reid stumbled into the street to escape, with Cornelison following him and now using a bullwhip to lash out at the defenseless man. What ensued in the following days would eventually destroy Richard Reid. Locals urged him

The case of Judge Richard Reid brought national attention to Kentucky's love of dueling.

to challenge his attacker to a duel; it was the only thing any honorable man could do, or so they thought. Reid decided otherwise. His religious beliefs prevented him from seeking out violence, and he chose instead to focus on his election campaign.

Pressure mounted as the media picked up the story. Soon, Reid was scorned for not living up to the code. While some thought that he did the right thing, others mocked him as a coward. At dinner one evening, one month after the attack, some claim that his wife placed a gun on the dinner table and told him to do what he must. One presumes she meant to take revenge against Cornelison. The next day, Reid went to a colleague's office and asked to lay down since he was feeling a little off-color. An hour later, he was dead from a shotgun wound to the head. In a biography of the judge, written two years after his death, Mrs. Reid mentioned that Cornelison was seen entering the office shortly before Reid's body was found. She also highlighted other evidence that she felt pointed to murder rather than suicide. Nevertheless, the court verdict reflected general opinion—that Judge Richard Reid had taken his own life. A statue at his grave faces with its back to the town, an expression of Mrs. Reid's contempt for the people who drove him to his death. Cornelison, expelled from his church, was later sentenced to three years for attacking the judge.

Since most Kentuckians carried knives or guns as a matter of daily business, and since laws preventing the carrying of concealed weapons were rarely enforced, the Code Duello provided a certain amount of restraint among gentlemen. The code laid down strict rules covering everything from who could fight a duel to where, when and how it should be conducted. Just as some behaviors would have been disgraceful and unbecoming of a knight, so were similar actions forbidden among gentlemen. Lorenzo Sabine outlined a list of "disgraces to dueling" that included the drawing of lots to decide weapons, the fighting between father and son and cheating by providing one loaded and one unloaded weapon. Some rules seem almost trivial, but they all played into the perceived role of a man in society. It was highly improper to fight naked (begging the question as to who would want to) or even shirtless. Swearing was unseemly, as was any form of celebration after a duel that resulted in a death. Finally, a truly honorable man would not insist on fighting a duel if his challenged opponent had made the proper forms of atonement, often some sort of public apology.

The General Assembly of Kentucky passed a law banning dueling in 1799. Among the punishments were fines, prison and disqualification from holding public office for seven years. The law proved to be ineffectual, however, since the defense of honor through violence was deeply rooted in the Kentucky mind.

As ritualized as the Code Duello was in theory, in practice the defense of one's name often proved to be little more than an excuse for bloodshed. Yet it was one that the people of Lexington, and of the state, understood and often excused, as seen in the case of Charles Wickliffe.

Charles Wickliffe

In 1829, Charles Wickliffe was a young man of twenty, keen to make his mark on the world. His father, Robert, was a cousin of the Todd family (into whom Abraham Lincoln would later marry) and the largest slave owner in the state. Charles, the eldest son, was keen to follow in his father's footsteps as a man of considerable economic and political clout. Sadly, young Charles had a bit of a temper.

When Thomas Benning entered the newspaper profession, he could have hardly suspected that he would find himself on the receiving end of such a temper. Orphaned as a child, Benning struggled to overcome the poverty that befell him. Remembering the advice given to him by his mother before her death, he worked hard and focused on his studies as a way to raise his rank in life. While teaching school in Winchester, he studied law and moved to Paris, Bourbon County, with the intent of practicing. Upon his arrival in the town, however, he was offered the position of editor of the *Paris Advertiser*. After displaying considerable promise there, Benning took up the invitation to move to Lexington and take over the running of the *Kentucky Gazette*.

Benning was a liberal, a keen supporter of education and local farmers and a vocal opponent of unjust monopolies. At the same time, he was well liked in local circles, where his sincerity and integrity were admired. He was a firm believer in the power of the press as a voice for freedom. He also, perhaps rather innocently given the era, never carried a firearm. Had he done so, his fate might have been very different.

A letter, apparently by Wickliffe Sr. but signed "Coriolanus" (the legendary Roman leader), appeared in the *Kentucky Gazette*, complaining that the writers at the paper, especially Benning, seemed to be determined to heap abuse on him. Benning printed a response under the name "Dentatus" (the incorruptible hero of the Roman Republic). Young Charles seized on the opportunity to defend the family honor. Marching into the newspaper office with a friend, he demanded to know who had written such a scandalous piece. Benning refused to provide a name, and the friend, after reading both pieces, advised Charles to let things be. Wickliffe left but sent word later, demanding once more the identity of Dentatus. Finally, on March 9, 1829, he returned to the newspaper offices. Benning's walking cane proved a useless defense against the angry Wickliffe. He attempted to flee, but Charles Wickliffe shot him in the back. Thomas Benning died shortly after.

Although this may seem an obvious case of coldblooded murder, the courts of the day did not think so. Robert Wickliffe was great friends with lawyer and statesman Henry Clay (who would feature prominently in several other dueling cases). Clay successfully argued that the shooting was carried out to protect the family honor and therefore was self-defense. Remarkably, Charles Wickliffe was acquitted of murder after a jury deliberation of just seven minutes.

Although Wickliffe's influence had meant that local leaders sided with him, the townspeople were angered by his acquittal. The *Gazette* wrote, "It is the monstrous fact, that there are many persons in this place, of reputable standing in society, who justify the murder of Benning, and some who applaud it." All about town, people speculated that he had gotten away with murder simply because of whom his father was friends with, namely Henry Clay.

What happened to Charles? Fate decreed that his hotheadedness got the better of him once more. On September 28, 1829, he took offense to an editorial in the *Kentucky Gazette* that insinuated that Wickliffe had cowardly murdered Benning and then had cheated justice by loading the court with a "packed and perjured jury." Once more, he marched to the editorial offices to seek redress. This time the editor was James George Trotter, a good friend of his since childhood.

Despite their cordial (until now) relationship, Trotter stood by the content of his newspaper and refused to apologize. Tempers flared and Wickliffe challenged Trotter to a duel. Clearly, the role of *Kentucky Gazette* editor was becoming a rather dangerous career choice, especially while Charles Wickliffe had anything to do with it.

The two men met at the county line on the allotted day of October 9, 1829. Rather than firing from the customary thirty feet, they agreed to a mere eight feet. Both took aim, fired…and missed. Determined that any slurs to his honor be avenged, Wickliffe demanded the right to take a second shot. His opponent, equally unwilling to back down, shot back his response: "Sir, you shall have it with pleasure." With that, the two men aimed once more, and Trotter shot Wickliffe just above the hip. The wounded man died just three hours later.

Immediately, friends of the deceased began to speculate that the duel had not been proper and had instead broken the Code Duello, something that those present keenly denied. Trotter continued his tenure at the *Gazette* for another four years, but some say that he never recovered from the horror of killing a man.

COLONELS GREEN AND BALDWIN

Writing for the press was a dangerous profession in days gone by; one never knew when someone might take offense at what you had written. Whereas today, disagreement over an editorial might result in a few harsh words on a blog, in nineteenth-century Lexington, it might result in dueling to the death. You had to be ready to fight with a weapon as well as with words—the pen was not always mightier than the sword.

Colonel Thomas Green was a correspondent for the *Cincinnati Commercial-Gazette*. In August 1887, he wrote an editorial accusing Colonel Lew Baldwin of falsifying voter records to ensure his election as deputy collector of internal revenue in Jessamine County. Baldwin responded in the only way a gentleman could—by challenging Green to a duel in Cincinnati. However, fate would intervene before the niceties of the Code Duello could be performed.

On November 16, Colonel Green was visiting Lexington for the unveiling of a statue of John C. Breckinridge. Little did he know that Colonel Baldwin also happened to be in town. The two men met on Main Street, just outside the Phoenix Hotel. Upon recognizing Green, Baldwin began to yell insults and demanded that the journalist apologize for the comments he had made in print. Some bystanders would later claim that Green was rather deaf and so did not hear the threats made against him.

Rather he continued on his way, perhaps blissfully unaware of the verbal abuse being hurled in his direction. Thinking that he had been ignored, Colonel Baldwin grabbed the newsman and a scuffle ensued. As they grappled with each other, Baldwin drew his pistol, smacking Green about the head and firing at him. The quick-thinking writer returned fire, hitting Baldwin twice; the wounds were fatal. The journalist was wounded by minor gunshots to the rib and above his eye. A nearby editor who tried to intervene (no doubt in his own attempt to experience the deadly nature of his profession) received two gunshots to the wrist.

THE GOODLOE AND SWOPE CASE

Perhaps one of Lexington's most famous duels, the encounter between William Goodloe and Armistead Swope took place sixty years after the Charles Wickliffe tragedy.

William Cassius Goodloe was born in Madison County in 1841. He came from a family with a proud military and political history; his great-grandfather had fought in the Revolutionary War, and his grandfather was a congressman. He was also related to the Clay family. Educated in local private schools and then Transylvania University, William withdrew from education to serve briefly as secretary to Cassius Clay in Russia. Upon returning to the United States in 1862, he joined the Union army and served for two years. His military career was not distinguished, and he never rose above the rank of captain. However, he took the honorary title of colonel, married and opened a law practice in Lexington. Goodloe was also the agent in charge of the Freedmen's Bureau in Mercer, Boyle and Lincoln Counties.

By 1867, he had become a key member in the local Republican Party and began publishing a local newspaper, the *Kentucky Statesman*. He ran for various offices, but with the exception of a few years in the state Senate, he met with little success. He served as the minister to Belgium for two years before returning to Kentucky in 1880 and focusing on local politics. Goodloe may have had little political success, but he was a keen public speaker. He was also regarded as rather arrogant, with "a bitter tongue," something that made him many enemies both within his own party and elsewhere. One such enemy was Colonel Armistead M. Swope.

Colonel Swope—killed by William Cassius Goodloe in the Lexington Post Office. *Courtesy of University of Kentucky, Gay Robinson Collection.*

Swope, described by some as "a large man with a splendid physique," was Goodloe's rival for leadership of the Republican Party. A lawyer in Paris, Kentucky, he had relocated to Lexington upon his appointment as an internal revenue collector by President Chester Arthur. In 1888, the rivals had clashed at the Republican State Convention as they argued which of them should be the delegate to the National Convention in Chicago. A few days later, the two met in Lexington's Phoenix Hotel. Swope "denounced Goodloe for everything he could think of."

For the next year or so, the rift appeared to be delicately but successfully patched up, thanks to the careful maneuvering of mutual friends. The two may have even retracted their insults toward each other, albeit in writing rather than in person. However, it was a fragile peace that would not last. Each man reputedly confided in those close to them. Swope felt that something must be done about Goodloe, lest he be seen a coward, the most egregious insult to a Bluegrass gentleman. Goodloe sought advice from his great uncle Cassius Clay, a man known for his fiery temper and love of the blade. According to one story, Cassius gave him a knife from his own collection. The knife was later described as "a terrible weapon, sharpened to a razor's edge on both sides of the point, with a blade five inches long and with a rough bone grip handle." Clay warned his nephew, "If Armistead Swope insults you again and you don't kill him, you're no Clay. I never want to see you again." The stage had been set.

So it was that the two men met, by chance, in the Lexington Post Office on Friday, November 8, 1889. In a scene that would be almost comical were it not so tragic, Swope and Goodloe were collecting their mail. As it happened, their mailboxes were next to each other. Goodloe accused his rival of obstructing his way. Swope responded with the charge that Goodloe had insulted him by the very act of speaking. In a flash, both men drew their weapons: Swope his .38-caliber Smith & Wesson, Goodloe the large dirk given to him by his uncle. Swope fired twice, but Goodloe stabbed him an impressive thirteen times, killing him on the spot.

With a bullet wound to the abdomen, Colonel Goodloe was carried to the Phoenix Hotel, where he died two days later. His Uncle Cass cried upon news of his death but proclaimed him a true Clay with the words, "I couldn't have done better myself."

The *Lexington Leader* reported that news of the events spread like wildfire through the city. Eyewitnesses told of the events, while crowds gathered at the post office to see the bloody scene for themselves.

At Swope's funeral, friends revealed that he had spoken previously of his disdain for Goodloe but had discarded all weapons since he thought highly of Mrs. Goodloe and had no desire to make her a widow. He had taken to carrying the Smith & Wesson with him once more because he intended to use it against another enemy, Preston Kimball, who had called Swope "the ass of the desert."

What became known as the Lexington Tragedy shocked not just the state but the entire nation, and it served as evidence of the "disgraceful and fatal defect" in Kentucky's civilization. Just two years earlier, the *New York Times* had suggested that the people of Kentucky needed "to be educated in the principles of civilized humanity." Now, the *Chicago Tribune* asked what sort of place would drive two well-educated men of exemplary character to carry weapons and "rush at each other like two savages." The article concluded that Kentuckians relied on the savagery of the Indian days rather than taking the morally superior route of rising above violence. The *Louisville Courier-Journal* retaliated, arguing that certain times arose when it was necessary to face one's critics and that there was scarcely evidence of greater morality in the North, where material wealth was apparently a measure of success.

DUELING DOCTORS

One likes to think of doctors as learned individuals, devoted to the healing arts and to saving the lives of others—hardly the sort of gents to be trying to kill one another, even in the name of honor. Yet that is precisely what happened in 1818 in what may be Kentucky's only pair of dueling doctors.

It seems that there was quite a rivalry between Lexington doctors back in the early nineteenth century. Drs. Daniel Drake, Benjamin Dudley and William Richardson all taught at the Transylvania Medical School and practiced locally.

Daniel Drake had grown up in poverty, but despite limited schooling, he showed great aptitude and was the first person west of the Alleghenies to be granted a medical diploma. He taught briefly at Transylvania before moving to Cincinnati, where he established the Medical College of Ohio in 1819 and the State Lunatic Asylum in 1820. Drake's studies of inland diseases helped to mark him as one of the foremost physicians of his time. He spent his career moving between Kentucky and Ohio, and the frequency of his relocations might suggest a man who had a penchant for making enemies.

Professional rivalry as to who was the better doctor grew into serious animosity when Drake published a pamphlet referring to Dudley as "an ignoramus, bully and a liar." Dudley had objected to Richardson's presence on the faculty as a professor of obstetrics on the grounds that he lacked a medical degree. He was also incensed by Drake's decision to resign after only one year on the faculty (Drake had originally promised to remain for at least two).

Things reached critical point when Drake and Dudley were called to perform an autopsy on a local man. Drake promptly announced that he was going fishing, leaving Dudley to do the postmortem, only to return and announce that the doctor's report as to cause of death was wrong. Further, he argued that Dr. Dudley lacked honor and integrity.

Dr. Daniel Drake ignored a challenge from Dr. Benjamin Dudley, but someone else was willing to take his place. *Courtesy of National Library of Medicine.*

Benjamin Dudley had been educated at Transylvania and the University of Pennsylvania. Just a few years earlier, he had returned from four years of medical study in Europe, where he had been admitted to the Royal College of Surgeons. In 1817, he was appointed head of the Transylvania Medical Department and chair of anatomy and surgery. Dudley specialized in bladder surgery but also became known as a pioneer in neurosurgery. Revered in the local community, he was considered somewhat distant. The European mannerisms he had acquired made him stand out from those around him. Perhaps this rather privileged background contributed to the tension between Dudley and Drake. Whatever the case, this fine doctor could no longer stand the abuse to his honor, and he challenged Drake to a duel. In rather an odd move, given the usual brand of cowardice to anyone who ignored a challenge, Drake refused to accept. Richardson, angered by Dudley's attitude toward his own medical skills and lack of formal training, stepped in and said that he would fight instead.

The two men met in the grounds surrounding the Abraham Buford House at the allotted time. The Buford House appears to have been a popular spot; it was also the site of the Wickliffe-Trotter duel. The two doctors raised their weapons and took the required number of paces before turning to fire. Richardson missed, but his challenger shot him in the groin. Blood flowed as Richardson's personal doctor tried in vain to plug the wound. Dudley, man of medicine that he was, walked over and offered his assistance. He stopped the bleeding while the other doctor tied off the blood vessel.

Back in Lexington, people were horrified by the thought of doctors participating in such an activity. Only the influence of Henry Clay (himself a dueler, as we shall see) could prevent them being expelled from their local Masonic chapter. Eventually, as with all such affairs, the furor died down. The men all went on to become great friends, despite having once tried to kill each other. In 1819, upon Drake's recommendation, Richardson received an honorary medical degree from the College of Physicians and Surgeons in New York.

TWENTIETH CENTURY DUEL

There is even a rare incidence of a call to arms for a duel in 1901. Desha Breckinridge, the son of Colonel William Breckinridge (whose fall from grace we shall read about in the fourth chapter), was an attorney and the editor of the *Lexington Herald*. He took offense when during the 1900 election, Patrick T. Farnsworth, the editor of a competing Lexington newspaper (the *Argonaut*), voiced his support of a presidential candidate. Breckinridge claimed that some of the comments made were insulting. He reportedly approached Farnsworth, calling him a liar, and drew his pistol. Someone struck Farnsworth on the back of the head. The man then claimed that an angry mob would have harmed Breckinridge had he not pleaded with them to stop. On a later occasion, the two met in the Phoenix Hotel. Farnsworth claimed that Breckinridge rushed toward him in such a manner that he was sure that danger would come to him, but again nothing came of it.

Some time later, the editor of the *Argonaut* moved to accept a newspaper position in New York. Desha Breckinridge took the opportunity to brag that

Desha Breckinridge, the quick-tempered son of Colonel W.P. Breckinridge, was married to leading Kentucky reformer, Madeline McDowell.

he had fled Lexington because he feared the mighty Breckinridges—hence the challenge to a duel.

For all the fighting words, the challenge came to naught. Breckinridge declared that he had not made the alleged statements. Furthermore, he did not take the challenge seriously, and given his career as a lawyer, he would not entertain the idea of accepting.

The days of the dueling gentlemen of Lexington may be over, but they live on in the oath required of all politicians and notaries in the state. All people taking an oath of office in Kentucky are required to recite the following:

> *I, being a citizen of this State, have not fought a duel with deadly weapons within this State nor out of it, nor have I sent or accepted a challenge to fight a duel with deadly weapons, nor have I acted as second in carrying a challenge, nor aided or assisted any person thus offending, so help me God.*

Chapter 2

THE LION AND THE COMPROMISER

DUELING CLAYS

CASSIUS MARCELLUS CLAY

Since his role in the Goodloe-Swope encounter has already been mentioned, it would be remiss not to include a further look at one of central Kentucky's most impassioned characters. A staunch antislavery campaigner, a publisher who had to barricade the doors to his office for protection and a minister to Russia, as notable for his personal life as for his professional accomplishments, Cassius Marcellus Clay, also known as the Lion of White Hall, continues to hold a fascination for many locals.

Clay was born in 1810 in neighboring Madison County. His father, General Green Clay, was a wealthy landowner and slaveholder and an early settler in Kentucky. Mother Sallie was a strict Calvinist Baptist. After attending Lexington's Transylvania University, Cassius continued his studies at Yale, where he was exposed to the views of abolitionist William Lloyd Garrison. He was greatly moved by Garrison's speeches. From then on, he became a strong opponent of slavery. There were two schools of thought among those devoted to ending slavery. Abolitionists were willing to use any means necessary to end the institution, while emancipationists wanted to bring about an end to slavery through the law. Clay, although far more outspoken than some fellow emancipationists, continued to believe in the potential for change within the law and the Constitution. Originally, like his cousin Henry Clay, Cassius favored the colonial point of view—that slaves,

Cassius Clay, in his younger but no less eccentric days. *Courtesy of Library of Congress.*

once emancipated, should be repatriated in Africa to live separately from whites. In time, however, his viewpoint changed, and he believed that they should be free to live where they chose.

Fresh from Yale, Cassius Clay returned to Lexington, where he reenrolled at Transy and earned his law degree. He also married Mary Jane Warfield. The couple would go on to have ten children, of which six survived. With law degree in hand, he decided to enter the political arena. In 1835, he was elected Madison County's state representative. Although he was defeated in 1836, he was reelected the following year. Oratorical skills apparently ran in the Clay genes, and Cassius was often praised for his speeches. Nevertheless, he was an emancipationist in slave country. This made him less than popular, and that is where Clay's skills as a fighter and dueler came in handy.

At the time of his death, the *New York Times* claimed that Cassius Clay had fought in more duels and killed more men than any other man alive. Clay would no doubt have been pleased to hold such an honor. As an old man, he was covered in scars, reminders of his many encounters. He said that his first challenge was for the hand of his wife Mary Jane. Another suitor, Dr. John Declarey, wrote to her father, arguing that Clay was not a suitable match. Indeed, he charged that Clay had ruined the reputation of another local woman, who had been forced to flee to Texas to avoid the shame. Clay tracked down the man and gave him a good whipping. He then issued a challenge to duel, but his opponent committed suicide, slitting his own throat. Declarey's fate caused Clay to muse, "I never could understand how a man could have the nerve to kill himself and yet show too much cowardice to fight."

Clay challenged Robert Wickliffe to a duel, accusing the latter of insulting Mrs. Clay. Both fired, but their shots missed and the seconds put an end to the matter. Shortly after, he received a letter from his mother begging him not to fight another duel. He would only fight one more during his lifetime, while serving in the Mexican-American War. That doesn't mean that he didn't issue multiple challenges or engage in bloodshed, though. In 1843, an assassin by the name of Samuel Brown was hired (some say by Wickliffe) to kill Cassius Clay and shot him in the chest. Clay fought back with his weapon of choice, a Bowie knife, causing serious injury to Brown. As for the bullet to the chest, it failed to penetrate after being blocked by Clay's knife scabbard. A piece of luck indeed.

Things didn't always go so well for him. In 1849, he was beaten by a crowd as he left the podium after delivering an antislavery speech. One member of the crowd had called him a liar, at which point he drew his knife. The crowd disarmed him and began attacking him. During the fracas, he was stabbed in the lung. Not one to let a mere punctured lung stop him, Clay fought, wrestling his knife back (even though it meant slicing through his own fingers) and stabbing the man who had insulted him. Clay's son, Warfield, who was fourteen at the time and accustomed to his father's penchant for trouble, handed his dad a pistol just as another proslaver tried to shoot him in the head. The opponent's gun misfired. Clay passed out from loss of blood. Before he did so, he uttered what he believed would be his dying words: "I died in the defense of the liberties of the people." As commendable as his urge to be remembered uttering words of wisdom might be, Cassius did not die. After a few months of rest, he was back to his old fiery ways. He was charged in the incident, but Henry Clay successfully defended him. In return, Cassius would show his gratitude by speaking in support of his cousin's presidential election bid in 1844. That didn't go so well either. Henry asked him to tone down the antislavery rhetoric, a move that alienated abolitionists who wanted more fire. Clay lost the election to James Polk, a proslavery Southerner.

Although the family home of White Hall was located in Madison County, Cassius and his family spent a great deal of time living in Lexington. In 1845, Cassius launched the only antislavery newspaper in the South, the *True American*. It was an unpopular move, as one letter to the newspaper showed:

> *You are meaner than the autocrats of hell. You may think you can awe and curse the people of Kentucky to your infamous course. You will find, when it is too late for life, the people are no cowards. Eternal hatred is locked up in the bosoms of braver men, your betters, for you. The hemp is ready for your neck. Your life cannot be spared. Plenty thirst for your blood—are determined to have it. It is unknown to you and your friends, if you have any, and in a way you little dream of.*
>
> *(signed) Revengers*

It seems inappropriate to use the word "fear" in the same sentence as Cassius Clay, so out of concern for the safety of his family and his newspaper, Clay replaced the doors to his office with iron ones and reportedly placed a cannon inside, lest he should find himself under attack. Elsewhere in town, a "committee of sixty" conspired to put an end to the *True American*. While Clay was ill, Henry's son, James, filed an injunction against the newspaper, broke into the offices and sent the printing equipment to Cincinnati. (Needless to say, this strained family relations). Typhoid and a stabbing had not stopped the Lion of White Hall, and neither would a relocation of office supplies. The *True American* continued, printing in Cincinnati with a Lexington dateline. Several years later, Cassius won a legal settlement against James and was awarded damages.

The next year, Cassius served in the Mexican-American War. In spite of earlier opposition to the action, his decision to serve was designed to boost his political status among those in his home state. It worked. He returned to a hero's welcome in Lexington, and the people who previously had sought to drive him from the city presented him with a Tiffany sword as a reward for bravery. Incidentally, during his time away, he challenged longtime enemy Tom Marshall to a duel. Apparently familiar with Clay's reputation, Marshall drowned himself.

Over the next decade, Clay continued to speak against slavery and helped to establish Berea College. During one speech in Springfield, Illinois, he met and befriended another Kentuckian and frequent visitor to Lexington, Abraham Lincoln. Lincoln and Clay would spend many hours discussing emancipation. When elected president, Lincoln thanked Clay for his support by appointing him minister to Russia. He spent two years in the court of the tsar and then returned to Washington to become a major general. He continued to speak for emancipation, so when Lincoln signed the Emancipation Proclamation in 1863, Clay saw it as "the culminating act of my life's aspirations."

Clay returned to Russia in 1863. In 1867, he was responsible, in part, for the purchase of Alaska. He returned to White Hall in 1869 to pursue a rather eccentric retirement. Increasingly paranoid, he placed firearms around White Hall to protect himself against his enemies, even going so far as to line up a cannon aimed through a porthole toward the main approach to the house. He abandoned the Republican Party to become a Democrat and divorced Mary Jane after forty-five years of marriage. The decision, which estranged him from his children, was based on his love of Tolstoy's works. He became convinced that he should be married not to an aristocrat but rather to a "daughter of the people." No doubt his love of young girls also played a part—he later admitted to having fallen deeply in love with several young women while still married, all barely fifteen. When he was eighty-three, he remarried, but the partnership with a fifteen-year-old servant's daughter was doomed to failure and lasted only one year. He attempted to educate his "peasant wife," but she repeatedly ran away. Finally, he filed for divorce on the grounds of abandonment. One week after the divorce was granted, he took out an ad in the *New York Journal* looking for a wife.

Clay remained ready for a fight to the end. In 1886, he published his memoirs. One line refers to his marriage to Mary Jane: "[M]y love for her was pure and devoted, and it was she who made the first breach upon the marriage duties." When one New York reviewer, Julian Hawthorne (son of writer Nathaniel), suggested that Mrs. Clay had been unfaithful, Cassius leapt to the defense of his former wife and challenged Hawthorne to a duel.

The reviewer apologized and the matter was dropped. Local lore also tells that a neighbor challenged him to a duel. Clay, well into his eighties, agreed but then declined because "if he kills me, it would be a good man gone." When men attempted to break into his house, the elderly man, riddled with gout, still managed to shoot one intruder and fatally stab another in the belly.

Cassius Marcellus Clay died on July 22, 1903. He is buried in Richmond, not far from his family home. In 2000, he was inducted into the Kentucky Commission on Human Rights' Civil Rights Hall of Fame.

HENRY CLAY: THE DUELING STATESMAN

Even Lexington's most illustrious statesman was not above pistols and ten paces when he felt it necessary to defend his honor.

The Great Compromiser, as Henry Clay would become known during his lifetime, was born in Hanover County, Virginia, in 1777. One of nine children, he grew up in a rural, slaveholding part of the country, an area that was home to numerous political leaders, including Patrick Henry of "Give me liberty, or give me death!" fame. After the death of his father, his mother married Captain Henry Watkins, and through this connection the young Henry Clay was able to get work as a clerk. Perhaps it was this experience that provided him with the impetus to become a lawyer. In 1797, with law license in hand, Henry Clay set out to seek his fortunes in the new lands of Kentucky. He established an office in Lexington and quickly became known as a brilliant legal mind and a highly capable trial attorney.

The year 1803 ushered in the beginning of Henry Clay's political career with his election to the Kentucky General Assembly. Just three years later, he was appointed to the United States Senate. In the following years, Clay would serve as the commissioner to negotiate peace with the British, support Latin-American independence, oppose the Mexican-American War and broker the Missouri Compromise. He was a principal political opponent of Andrew Jackson and made several unsuccessful bids for the American presidency. At the same time, he built the magnificent Ashland estate in Lexington, where he escaped the hustle and bustle of Washington life to spend time with his wife, Lucretia, and their children. When Clay died of tuberculosis in 1852, he was the first person to lie in state in the capitol rotunda. A huge procession

Henry Clay, aka the Great Emancipator—lawyer, politician and beloved son of Lexington. *Courtesy of Library of Congress.*

made its way back to Lexington, and an estimated 100,000 people lined the streets for his funeral. (Remember that at this time, Lexington's population was little more than 9,000.) The monument at his tomb in the Lexington Cemetery still towers above the surrounding graves, a life-size statue of the man looking across the town he loved so much.

Henry Clay fought two duels in his lifetime. The first was in 1809, when he faced off against political nemesis Humphrey Marshall. At the time, Clay was a member of the Kentucky House of Representatives. Marshall, a Revolutionary War veteran who had moved to Kentucky in 1781, was a fellow member of the House. The two had been on ill terms ever since Clay had served as chief counsel for Aaron Burr's trial in 1806. Burr had been indicted by the U.S. district attorney for planning an illegal expedition into Spanish territory. Clay successfully defended him and was able to get a judge to throw the charges out. Humphrey Marshall wrote a scathing criticism of Clay in the Frankfort newspaper, *Western World*. In 1808, Marshall found himself the sole Federalist in the House. Worse still, his desk was nearly next to that of Clay. All that separated the pair was a German immigrant named Christopher Riffe.

Clay sponsored a bill in December 1808 proposing a trade embargo against France and England. Marshall was the lone opposition as the bill passed sixty-four to one. Apparently, by this time, tensions between the two provided a certain amount of entertainment for the other members of the House, who would watch to see how soon tempers would flare. They did not have to wait much longer.

Clay was known for his finely tailored English suits. However, as political relations with England became more strained, and once the trade embargo was passed, the politician decided to make an obvious gesture to show his support for American industry. He introduced the Homespun Resolution, calling upon legislators to wear only American-produced cloth. He emphasized his support of the bill by wearing a suit made of homespun denim. Marshall decided to reiterate his support for English trade, and the next day, he strode into chambers wearing fine imported broadcloth. Clay disparaged Marshall's lack of patriotism. And then fists, as well as accusations, began to fly.

As fellow legislators struggled to keep the two apart, Christopher Riffe placed himself between the men, ordering them to stop or he would give them both a good whipping. The weakest of apologies were offered, but they did nothing to appease either man. Doing what any gentleman would do when his honor was questioned, Clay challenged Marshall to a duel.

Henry Clay's dueling pistols remain on display at Ashland. These were not used in either of the duels he fought. *Courtesy of Ashland, the Henry Clay estate.*

Dueling may have been banned in the state of Kentucky in 1799, but that failed to stop even the most proper of politicians when honor was at stake. On January 19, 1809, the two crossed the river into Indiana, thus placing themselves out of state jurisdiction. Marshall's first shot missed, while Clay's skimmed his opponent, providing only a small wound. They fired again and each missed. In the third round, Clay missed but Marshall hit him in the thigh. At this point, the seconds stepped in, refusing Clay's demands for a fourth shot. The matter was finished, although historians have since referred to the duel as one of Kentucky's "great historical what-ifs." Had Clay been killed by Marshall, several major events in American history might well have taken a very different path. Would the Missouri Compromise have passed? Would the negotiations after the War of 1812 have turned out differently? Would the Civil War have come earlier? An alternative political environment, one without the Great Compromiser, might have taken American history down a very different path.

A second duel took place in 1826. This time, Clay was serving as the U.S. secretary of state. John Randolph, a U.S. senator from Virginia, made a number of attacks against Clay and John Quincy Adams on the floor of Congress, culminating in one that implied Clay to be a blackleg (slang for a card cheat). Since he was not present at the time and therefore unable to defend his reputation, he felt that he had no choice but to challenge Randolph to a duel. In his autobiography *Thirty Years View*, Missouri senator Thomas Hart Benton wrote of the affair: "Never, in my judgment, has the utter, unconditional absurdity and folly of dueling been so profoundly demonstrated, as in the case before us. These two great men…loved one another."

Folly it may well have been. Randolph approached Benton to be his second but was saddened to learn that he was related to Clay's wife, Lucretia. In truth, it seems unlikely that the Virginia man even wanted to duel; he had never before participated in any public gunplay. However, he felt that accepting the challenge was a must in order to preserve his honor and to safeguard the freedom to speak in the Senate without reprisals from members of the administration.

For his part, Benton begged Clay not to continue with his challenge. Lucretia had recently suffered the loss of two daughters, and her cousin did not wish any more grief to befall her. When it became clear that Clay intended to see it through, Benton approached Randolph. Randolph let it be

Senator John Randolph may have fought a duel with Henry Clay, but he preferred to keep his quarrels in the Senate. *Courtesy of Library of Congress.*

known that he had "determined upon receiving, without returning, Clay's fire; nothing shall induce me to harm a hair upon his head; I will not make his wife a widow or his children orphans."

The two met on the Virginia side of the Potomac at four o'clock on April 8, 1826. Randolph deliberately aimed low with his first shot, and in return, he received a torn trouser leg from his opponent. With his second shot, Clay sent a bullet through the fabric of Randolph's coat. Randolph fired his gun into the sky and declared that he would not fire at Mr. Clay. In a letter recounting the events, Captain Nathaniel Young recalls that after firing, the two men "shook hands—and thus ended the affair." Reportedly, Randolph told Clay that he now owed him a new coat, to which Clay replied by expressing his gratitude that the debt was not greater.

Fifteen years later, another duel seemed on the horizon when William King, a senator from Alabama, challenged Clay to a duel. The senate sergeant at arms promptly arrested him. After making formal apologies to each other on the senate floor, Clay and King shared a pinch of snuff, to the applause of all those present. Clay's dueling days were behind him.

Chapter 3

WICKED WOMEN

DID MRS. MULLIGAN POISON THE FISH?

Judge James Hillary Mulligan was a favorite Lexington son. His father was a prominent business owner, and after receiving his law degree from Transylvania University, James had a full career as an attorney, judge and politician. He served in the Kentucky House and Senate and then as consul general to the island nation of Samoa, before returning to a peaceful life of semiretirement in his hometown. His poem "In Kentucky" gained national recognition after the judge first recited it at a dinner in 1902. Among the poem's notable lines:

> *The sunshine's ever brightest*
> *   In Kentucky;*
> *The breezes whisper lightest*
> *   In Kentucky;*
> *Plain girls are the fewest,*
> *Maidens' eyes the bluest,*
> *Their little hearts are truest*
> *   In Kentucky.*
>
> *Orators are the grandest*
> *   In Kentucky;*
> *Officials are the blandest*

In Kentucky

The moonlight falls the softest,
In Kentucky.
The summer days come oftest,
In Kentucky.
Friendship is the strongest,
Love's light glows the longest
Yet, wrong is always wrongest,
In Kentucky.

Life's burdens bear the lightest,
In Kentucky.
The home fires burn the brightest,
In Kentucky.
While players are the keenest,
Cards come out the meanest,
The pocket empties cleanest,
In Kentucky.

The sun shines ever brightest,
In Kentucky.
The breezes whisper lightest,
In Kentucky.
Plain girls are the fewest,
Their little hearts are truest,
Maidens' eyes the bluest,
In Kentucky.

Orators are the grandest,
In Kentucky.
Officials are the blandest,
In Kentucky.
Boys are all the fliest,
Danger ever nighest,
Taxes are the highest,
In Kentucky.

The bluegrass waves the bluest,
In Kentucky.
Yet, bluebloods are the fewest,
In Kentucky.
Moonshine is the clearest,
By no means the dearest,
And yet, it acts the queerest,
In Kentucky.

The dove notes are the saddest,
In Kentucky.
The streams dance on the gladdest
In Kentucky.
Hip pockets are the thickest,
Pistol hands the slickest,
The cylinder turns the quickest,
In Kentucky.

The song birds are the sweetest,
In Kentucky.
The thoroughbreds are fleetest,
In Kentucky.
Mountains tower proudest,
Thunder peals the loudest,
The landscape is the grandest,
And politics — the damndest,
In Kentucky.

James H. Mulligan

COPYRIGHT BY E C KROPP CO. MILWAUKEE WIS

"In Kentucky," the famed poem by James Mulligan. *Courtesy of University of Kentucky.*

In Kentucky;
Boys are all the fliest,
Danger ever nighest,
Taxes are the highest
In Kentucky.

Judge Mulligan's first wife, Mary, died in 1876, leaving him to raise four children alone. Five years later, he remarried. With his second wife, Genevieve, he fathered another six children. Later in life, Genevieve would find herself labeled the wicked stepmother.

As the family sat down to dinner one September evening in 1904, young Dennis Mulligan was preparing to help himself to some of the delicious-looking salmon salad that was among the selection of dishes on the table. Suddenly, Louis Mitchell, one of the house servants, dashed across, imploring the young man not to eat any. A former slave, Louis had been with the Mulligan household for fifteen years, ever since the judge had used his influence to free the man from prison. He left the dining room, clutching the plate with the salad. Dennis followed him to the kitchen in time to prevent him from throwing away the fish.

At first, Louis said that he feared for the safety of the dish, claiming to have seen a strange man lurking in the kitchen. When questioned by police, he implicated Jim Mulligan, a son from the judge's first marriage. Jim reportedly convinced him to lace the fish with poison so that his stepmother would die. A laboratory test would later reveal that the salmon had been laced with strychnine, sufficient to kill fifty people.

At the time of the attempted murder, Jim Mulligan worked as a reporter for a journal in Chicago. He and his two sisters, Alice and Mollie, were estranged from their father. They felt that their rightful inheritance was being stolen from them by the second Mrs. Mulligan. Upon hearing of Louis Mitchell's accusations, the Mulligan son quickly returned to Lexington, proclaiming his innocence.

Trials for the two men began within a fortnight. Although the judge would not believe his son to be part of such a malicious plot, he soon changed his opinions after testimony began. The accused young man revealed how much he loathed his stepmother, accusing her of attempting to alienate the judge from his four children by Mary. He also argued that she had abused his sister Mollie. The family home, Maxwell Place, was built partly with funds from the first Mrs. Mulligan, yet Alice and Mollie were not even allowed to visit the house. Then, in an interesting twist, he stated that he would not reveal whom he suspected to be truly responsible for the crime. He may not have been willing to point the finger in the courtroom, but rumors soon began to spread around Lexington belittling Genevieve Mulligan and even going so far as to claim that she had pretended to poison the fish so that she might further distance the judge from his children by blaming them for the evil deed.

Was Mrs. Mulligan the wrongdoer here? Had she concocted a clever plot to make herself appear the victim? Of the judge's eldest four children, only one son, Louis, spoke on behalf of his stepmother, saying that there had been some tension in the past but that relations with her were now very cordial.

Needless to say, the elderly judge was outraged at such attempts to slander his beloved wife. In a statement issued to the press, he addressed the rumors:

There was never a greater or more cruel misconstruction. As to any complicity on the part of my wife…no shadow ever…entered my mind…She stood, and stands, in need of no defense or tactics of delay. The intimation that she…perpetrated or conspired the base theatrical attack is too vile, too dastardly, to deserve characterization…[W]herever the deserved brand of condemnation may fall, it will not be upon her.

Although he would later deny it, the local press also claimed that he referred to his son as a "recreant sot."

Regardless of what may or may not have been said, the grand jury was unable to find any direct evidence linking Jim to the crime, and all charges against him were dropped. Louis Mitchell was accused of being the sole instigator. However, the jury was unable to agree on a verdict when the case went to trial in 1905. A second trial was held later the same year, and in a move rather unusual when a black man was accused, the jury acquitted him of all charges. The case would soon be forgotten. Louis Mitchell faded into obscurity. Judge and Mrs. Mulligan lived the rest of their days at Maxwell Place, leaving this earth within ten days of each other in 1915.

CAROLINE TURNER

The story of Caroline Turner has been forgotten by all but a few local historians. She commands only a few lines in the *Lexington Herald*, but history books refer to her in connection with one "of the most gruesome episodes" in the city's history.

Caroline Augusta Sargent was born in Brownsville, Pennsylvania, in 1795. Her father was Winthrop Sargent. Part of a once wealthy shipping family, the Harvard-educated Winthrop fought in the Continental army during the American Revolution, receiving a commendation from none other than George Washington. After the war, finding his family fortune lost and facing various health problems, Winthrop was a founding member of the Ohio County Association, formed to settle the Northwest Territories. He also served as the acting governor of the territories. In 1789, he married Rowena Tupper, but she died in childbirth the following year.

Sarah Chapese was a New Jersey woman with a fierce Irish temper. Although married to a doctor, they separated and reunited several times. It is uncertain how she met Winthrop—it may have been through Winthrop seeking medical treatment from her husband. Whatever the case, letters from Winthrop to his sister indicate a series of meetings with Sarah, and by early 1795 she had moved in with him at his home in Cincinnati. The main impetus for their cohabitation appears to have been the fact that Sarah was pregnant. From the outset, the relationship was not a happy one; Sarah's temper and their different backgrounds caused ongoing tension. Arguments were a frequent occurrence even before Caroline was born at the end of the year.

The events of the next few years are vague. Winthrop repeatedly sought custody of the young Caroline. His sister, Judith, offered to care for her, but Sarah refused to hear of such a thing. Letters from Winthrop to Judith indicated that the relationship between he and Sarah had completely dissolved and that he was concerned that the child was suffering as a result.

In 1798, Winthrop moved to Natchez, Mississippi, and was appointed governor of the Mississippi territory. A few months later, he married a local widow, Mary McIntosh Williams. Still, he tried in vain to gain custody of Caroline from Sarah, who had also remarried by this time.

Finally, in 1802, Winthrop gained custody of Caroline, then seven years old. Records claim that she had been subjected to "uncommon calamities." Although there is no indication what these might have been, there is reason to speculate that drinking and violence on Sarah's part, as well as general neglect, may all have been a part of the young girl's childhood. The next fifteen years are largely undocumented. Did Caroline live in Boston with her aunt Judith? Or did she live in Natchez with her father's new family? Perhaps it was a combination of both.

On September 24, 1817, Caroline married Fielding Lewis Turner. Born in Virginia, Fielding Turner had moved to Lexington in 1786 at the age of twenty. He became the deputy clerk of Fayette County in 1796 and was admitted to the bar a few years later. In 1806, he moved to Natchez and later to New Orleans, where he owned a prosperous mercantile business and fought in the Battle of New Orleans. It is likely that Fielding met Caroline in Natchez. What is not known, however, is if her father knew that the marriage would take place. Winthrop and Fielding were firmly placed on opposite sides of the political fence, and the father most certainly did not approve. To Winthrop, his daughter's marriage was tantamount to treason. His new will in 1818 made no mention of Caroline; she was disinherited. Whether her marriage to an opponent of her father's was the result of youthful folly or an act of revenge for a painful childhood is lost to history. We do know that Caroline never reunited with the Sargent family. Winthrop died in 1820 on his way to Philadelphia, his sister Judith one month later.

Caroline's childhood was certainly not a happy one, and sadly, married life had its share of tragedies, too. The newlywed couple lived in New Orleans, where business prospered. Fielding was also appointed a criminal court judge. While living in Louisiana, Caroline gave birth to five children: James died at the tender age of one month and baby Caroline at sixteen months.

And so it was that in 1827, the family moved to Judge Turner's family farm in Lexington. The judge took up a position as trustee at Transylvania University, equal in reputation to Harvard at the time. Perhaps a new start would bring new fortune and happiness for Caroline. The young Mrs. Turner seems to have made a good impression in Lexington society, with one historian commenting: "Mrs. Turner was a lady of great beauty and vivacity...She was well educated, and accomplished, and dressed with great richness and taste."

A son, Fielding Jr., was born sometime after their arrival in Lexington. He also passed away, at the age of eleven months. Even more tragically, Lucius, aged two, and the six-month-old Augustus both died on the same day in 1833. Caroline Turner buried five of her eight children before their third birthdays.

Such loss would have taken its toll on any woman, and Caroline was no exception. Rumors of cruelty toward her slaves began to circulate, a cruelty that "violated even Kentucky standards" according to historian Jean Baker. Many have claimed that her vicious temper was the reason Fielding never sought higher political office. In 1837, while whipping a young slave boy, she became so enraged that she flung the child from a second-story window. Miraculously, the boy survived, but he was left severely crippled. After this, her husband apparently had her forcibly committed to the Lexington Lunatic Asylum, but she was released a few days later when doctors concluded that there was nothing wrong with her. A letter, dated 1839, from John Clarke of New York, discussed Mrs. Turner and his own recent trip to Lexington:

I repeatedly heard, while in Lexington, Kentucky, during the winter of 1836–7, of the wanton cruelty practiced by this woman upon her slaves, and that she had caused several to be whipped to death, but I never heard that she was suspected of being deranged, otherwise than by the indulgence of an ungoverned temper, until I heard that her husband was attempting to incarcerate her in the Lunatic Asylum…I heard the testimony on the trial…and no facts came out relative to her treatment of her slaves…Some days after…I was present in my brother's office, when Judge Turner…said, "That woman has been the immediate cause of the death of six of my servants."

Her descendants, however, feel that Caroline Turner has been much maligned. They claim that, far from abusing her slaves, she was in fact practicing simple household discipline and that there is no evidence, save anecdotal, of any violence on her part.

In 1843, Judge Fielding Turner died. His will gives credence to the reputation of his wife: "I have some slaves. I give them to my children, none of them are to go to the said Caroline, for it would be to doom them to misery in life and a speedy death."

The events of the following year ensured Caroline Turner her place in Lexington history. Through whatever means, Caroline was able to retain some slaves. Whether they were those formerly belonging to her husband or whether she obtained new ones is not known. An excerpt hidden away in the August 24, 1844 edition of the *Observer and Reporter Newspaper* of

The Eastern Lunatic Asylum was the second such institution in the nation and a forerunner of mental healthcare. *Courtesy of Lexington History Museum.*

Lexington reported the fate of Caroline: "Mrs. Turner was reproving…her carriage driver for some bad conduct the evening before, when he seized and strangled her, before she could be rescued from his murderous grasp."

Those who have written about the incident since have claimed that, being raised in Boston, Caroline had never been exposed to slavery and that when she came to Lexington and owned slaves, her latent brutality came to the surface. However, a family history argues that such claims of brutality have been heavily embellished. Further, her history of childhood trauma, parental rejection and the loss of her own children were all more than anyone could have borne.

The slave, Richard Moore, had been described thus at the time of his sale: "[A]bout 24 years of age…he is very sensible and plausible." Richard was captured in Scott County as he attempted to flee. Back in Lexington, he was tried and hanged for the murder of Caroline Turner. A newspaper report from Paris, Kentucky, claimed that he had previously been tried for

500 DOLLARS
··· REWARD!

R ANAWAY on Thursday (22d inst.) from the residence of Mrs. C. A. TURNER, a negro man by the name of

RICAHRD.

He is about 24 years of age, of yellow complexion, about 6 feet high. He can read and write, and is a very sensible and plausible negro. He was raised in Fleming county, Ky., by James Jones, who this year brought him to Lexington, and sold him. Mrs. TURNER was found STRANGLED in her house, and from all the circumstances it is believed Richard murdered her, as she was his mistress, and he left immediately after the occurrence.

The above reward will be given for his apprehension out of the State, or $300 if taken in the State, and, in either case, delivered at the Lexington Jail.

OSCAR TURNER.

Fayette county, Ky. aug 21. 33

Louisville Journal, Maysville Eagle, and Cincinnati Gazette copy to amount of $2 each, and ch. this office.

This runaway slave notice offered a $500 reward for the man who killed Caroline Turner. He was caught and hanged.

two attempted murders in Flemingsburg. Given the attitudes of the day, this is highly suspect. A slave would have been unlikely to receive a fair trial, even less to be acquitted of any such crime. He certainly would not have survived and then moved on to Lexington. Equally unlikely is that any newspaper or court would have held Mrs. Turner responsible for cruelty toward a slave.

Many years later, Kentucky author Robert Penn Warren included the story of Caroline Turner in his Pulitzer Prize–winning classic, *All the King's Men*. He offered the following explanation for her deeds:

> One lady said to me, "Mrs. Turner did not understand Negroes." And another, "Mrs. Turner did it because she was from Boston where the Abolitionists are." But I did not understand. Then, much later, I began to understand. I understood that Mrs. Turner flogged her Negroes for the same reason that the wife of my friend sold Phoebe down the river: she could not bear their eyes upon her. I understand, for I can no longer bear their eyes upon me.

Was Caroline Sargent Turner a victim of circumstance? Did she inherit some genetic trait of violence from her mother? Had the misery of her own childhood, followed by the tragic deaths of her children, led to some sort of breakdown that manifested in an attack against her slaves? Or did she somehow become a misunderstood figment of Lexington's history? We may never know.

BELLE BREZING

So who was the most wicked woman of Lexington? How about a woman who, in her own day, was both celebrated and reviled, a woman whose death was reported in *Time* magazine and a woman in whose honor an annual race is held in the city? It was none other than Madam Belle.

Mary Belle Cox was born on June 16, 1860, the illegitimate child of seamstress/prostitute Sarah Ann Cox. The following year, when Sarah Ann married, Mary Belle and her elder sister, Hester, took the surname Brezing. Their mother would change their name again a few years later when she filed for divorce from George Brezing and moved in with William McMeekin.

Belle Brezing at eight years old, already showing the defiance that would help her survive and succeed. *Courtesy of University of Kentucky, Belle Brezing Collection.*

That relationship did not work out either, and Mary Belle would be known as Miss Brezing for most of her life.

Life for young Belle was lonely. As the daughter of a prostitute, neighbors and the other children shunned her. At school, she quickly discovered that she could either hang her head in shame and live an exercise in humility, or she could proudly look everyone in the eye and refuse to be cowed. Either way, people had already made up their minds about her because of her parentage. Even at an early age, Belle was not one to be cowed. She chose the latter.

Such lack of humility shocked the people of Lexington. How dare this young girl—the daughter of a prostitute, perhaps destined to become one herself—act so proudly! With the benefit of hindsight, it is now incredibly sad to read of how the townsfolk treated Belle from an early age. At the age of twelve, Belle was seduced by a married man, local merchant Dionesio Mucci, who was three times her age. We can only speculate as to whether the relationship was truly consensual or whether it was a way for Belle to find some semblance of love and acceptance. Since twelve was the age of consent at the time, and Belle's background meant that people thought the worst of her, newspapers openly ridiculed her instead of considering her a child and Mucci a predator. The relationship with Mucci was ongoing two years later; a scrapbook that he gave her as a Valentine's gift remains in the archives at the University of Kentucky. At the same time, there is reason to suspect that she had several other sexual partners, including James Kenney and Johnny Cook. One possibility is that, treated as an outcast by everyone, Belle learned that sex was the one weapon she had that made her desirable and gave her power.

In 1875, barely fifteen, Belle discovered that she was pregnant, apparently by young Johnny Cook. One might expect her to marry the father, but when three months pregnant, she instead married James Kenney. The *Lexington Daily Press* openly mocked the ceremony with a wedding announcement that informed readers:

> *A marriage in the high life is reported between Miss Belle Breezing and Mr. James Kinney. The ceremony was performed at the residence of the bride's mother. It was brief but most significant, and performed in a manner so touching that it drew tears from the eyes of those who witnessed it. La Belle Breezing is no more. She is now Mistress Kinney.*

Even stranger, the two did not live together; Belle simply returned to her mother's home after the marriage ceremony. Nine days later, she apparently wrote a letter to Cook requesting a gun. Shortly after their meeting, Cook was found at the gate to her house, a bullet in his skull. Kenney immediately disappeared and would not return to Lexington for ten years. To add one final twist to the strange incident, some sources reported that Dionesio Mucci was the last person to see young Johnny alive. The death was ruled suicide, but rumors of murder spread like wildfire. Belle's notoriety was sealed.

The year 1876 was a year of challenges for Belle. Daisy May Kenney was born on March 14. Two months later, Sarah died, and Belle found herself

Above: The Mary Todd Lincoln House has been the home of a First Lady and a store, as well as the site of the brothel where Belle Brezing first worked. *Photo by Fiona Young-Brown.*

Left: Jennie Hill was the only madam for whom Belle Brezing ever worked. *Courtesy of University of Kentucky, Belle Brezing Collection.*

and her baby on the streets with nowhere to live. (Elder sister Hester had married in 1871.) Although the events of the next few years are vague, it seems likely that Belle, survivor that she was, took advantage of the few opportunities available to her, engaging in semiprostitution and taking work where she could find it. We next hear of Belle at Christmas 1879. The petite nineteen-year-old knocked on the door of Jennie Hill's bordello (located in what was formerly the home of the Todd family) and entered a life of professional prostitution. Belle knew what men liked, and she soon became the home's top earner, with bankers and politicians among her clients.

By July 1881, Belle decided that it was time to open her own house. She was a keen businesswoman and so rented a house on North Upper Street. In opening her own business, Belle joined such other local madams

Lottie Brown, another Lexington madam. *Courtesy of University of Kentucky, Belle Brezing Collection.*

as Lizzie Hill, Blanche Patterson, Barb Burnell and Mother Board. At the same time, she made the difficult choice to send Daisy May to live in an institution in Newport, northern Kentucky. Daisy suffered from mental retardation and would live the rest of her life in care, first in Newport and then in Detroit.

A few months later, Belle found herself pregnant once again. Abortion was unthinkable; Belle was a strict Catholic throughout her life and was still legally married to Kenney because of her religious beliefs. The baby was stillborn in July 1882.

Over the next few years, Belle built her business, buying property on North Upper and making frequent visits to Cincinnati and New York, where she would purchase fine linens, furnishings and clothing. Since the best clientele could be found among the wealthiest citizens of Lexington, Belle was determined to own the fanciest bordello in town, with only the finest surroundings and entertainment. One of her patrons, William Singerly of Philadelphia, helped her to buy property on Megowan Street, in the city's red-light district. The house became the most stylish and the most orderly disorderly house in town. When fire badly damaged the house in 1895, restoration began immediately, and the house was soon back in business and better than ever.

Belle treated her girls well, often taking them to enjoy an afternoon at the opera or at the races. She taught her girls to behave well in public and to hold their heads high, as she had done since her first day at school. The Main Street department stores would open especially for her, so that she could take her girls to buy the finest new clothes. In return, those who worked for her followed the strict rules of the house: no visitors during the daytime, conservative dress and formal evening gowns during hours of business.

The madam's kindness was offered to anyone who needed it. In Buddy Thompson's biography of Belle, he quotes John Coyne, a bartender who worked for her: "For every bad thing Belle did, she did five hundred good ones." As an example, in 1911, when Debbie Harvey, a local working girl, was murdered, Belle ensured that she received a proper burial at the Lexington Cemetery. Brezing's generosity was not limited to those in her service, either. When a local hospital suffered a fire, she bought every set of sheets in stock at the local stores and had them sent to the hospital to replace what had been lost. Sadly, reputation trumped care, and the nurses returned them all once

Belle Brezing's fame spread across the nation. *Courtesy of University of Kentucky, Belle Brezing Collection.*

they learned the source of the donation. Better to let patients go without than to be sullied by one enmeshed in a life of sin.

Back at Megowan Street, Belle's guests were subject to the same combination of generosity and strictness. Any guests who became overly loud or unruly were escorted from the premises, while those who held a certain amount of influence were allowed to sleep off their drunkenness and

LUKE P. BLACKBURN

GOVERNOR OF THE COMMONWEALTH OF KENTUCKY.

TO ALL WHO SHALL SEE THESE PRESENTS, GREETING :

WHEREAS, *An indictment has been rendered by the Grand Jury for* Fayette *County,* Dec 14ᵗʰ *, 1882, against* Belle Brezing *for*

—— *Keeping a bawdy House* ——

NOW KNOW YE, *That by virtue of the power vested in me by the Constitution, I do by these presents* REMIT *said* indictment *and* PARDON *the* OFFENSE *as therein alleged, except commissions, fees, and costs, and do hereby forever acquit, release, and discharge said* Belle Brezing *as aforesaid, from the same, enjoining all officers to respect this* PARDON *and govern themselves accordingly.*

IN TESTIMONY WHEREOF, I, hereto, sign my name, and cause the seal of the Commonwealth to be affixed. Done at Frankfort, this 7ᵗʰ *day of* February *A. D. 188*3*.*

Luke P Blackburn

BY THE GOVERNOR:

James Blackburn
SECRETARY OF STATE

By ....

ASSISTANT SECRETARY OF STATE

The governor's declaration pardoning Belle Brezing from all charges of running a disorderly house. The madam never spent a night in jail, despite being the most indicted person in the city.

then were fed a hearty breakfast and sent home discreetly before the rest of the world awoke.

Her clientele certainly did hold influence. Some of the state's most powerful men crossed the brothel's threshold—bankers, politicians and businessmen. Belle's large personal fortune and investment savvy is said to be a result of her connections with those in the financial industry. They advised; she listened and reaped excellent dividends. Her political contacts also paid off. Belle was smart enough to make significant monetary donations to both sides of the political fence. After all, one never knows when one may need to call upon a favor from those in power. During her career, Belle Brezing was indicted more times than any other Lexington citizen, but she never served even one night behind bars. She paid fines promptly (the cost of doing business). She even received a governor's pardon after her first arrest in December 1882. Incidentally, that was her only charge of operating a bawdy house. Other charges filed over the years focused on the illegal sale of liquor.

Belle's long-term companion, Billy Mabon, in her parlor. *Courtesy of University of Kentucky, Belle Brezing Collection.*

When soldiers were stationed in Lexington for the Spanish-American War at the end of the century, they all wanted to visit Miss Belle's place—such was her nationwide reputation.

THE CRUSADE AGAINST VICE

The late nineteenth and early twentieth centuries saw a rise in concern about public morality. Repeated outbreaks of cholera and tuberculosis in larger cities turned people's attention to a need for better sanitation. At the same time, there was an increase in awareness of venereal disease. The two issues combined into an overall focus on health and, in turn, morality. Prostitution and vice were symbols of moral and social decay.

In 1900, New York magistrate Joseph Deuel collected and analyzed crime statistics from one hundred American cities in an attempt to define the most wicked cities in the nation. Including figures for *malum in se* (that which is considered inherently evil; murder, for example), assault, gambling, disorderly houses, vagrancy and disorderly conduct, he concluded that cities in the South were far more wicked than either Chicago or New York. Norfolk, Virginia, was branded the most wicked city in the United States. It was followed by two cities of extreme wickedness: Savannah, Georgia, and Lexington, Kentucky. Those seeking a less wicked environment should seek out Dubuque, Iowa; Allegheny, Pennsylvania; or Rhode Island (the lowest scorers in the poll). While another Kentucky city (Covington) ranked highly for gambling, Lexington was a pit of vice.

With many neighboring cities (Louisville, Knoxville, Cincinnati and so on) closing their red-light districts, there was an influx of women to the brothels in Lexington, all seeking work. Business was booming. By 1914, the problem of vice had become so great that a Vice Commission was formed to investigate the proliferation of prostitution within the city of Lexington and to propose solutions. The commission was composed of two members of the clergy, an attorney, a physician and several representatives of the local business community. There were two women in the group: one from the Kentucky Federation of Women's Clubs' Social Hygiene Department, and the vice-president of the local Orphan's Association. The following year, the commission released a report of its findings.

The commission members acknowledged a certain amount of opposition to their work, not only from those who made their livelihood through vice or some connection to it but also from those who felt that drawing attention to the city's less savory aspects would sully the good name of Lexington. In answer to their opponents, they stated the importance of seeking solutions rather than denying the existence of a problem: "Even misguided effort is better than to make no effort at all." They invited experts from the American Social Hygiene Association to Lexington so that they might discuss options and learn from their advice. Then it was time to evaluate the situation by doing a detailed survey of conditions in the city.

Although sight of such well-to-do gents as those in the commission may not have seemed out of the ordinary in the vice district (remember that Belle Brezing's clientele included the crème of the business world), the addition of the two ladies and members of the clergy must have been an odd sight as the commission visited twenty eight "parlor houses" (the polite term for the brothels) that lay in the block encompassed by what is now Wilson Street, Eastern Avenue and East Short Street. They estimated the parlors to house 131 inmates, although they noted that there were more than 160 registered prostitutes in the area, according to the local white slave officer. In addition, they visited twenty-two assignation houses (outside the district, where single rooms are used for prostitution) and twenty-seven parlor houses outside the district. Further, several investigators were solicited to go to hotel rooms. The survey concluded that there were greater numbers of parlor houses and prostitutes within Lexington than there were in Richmond, Virginia, even though the overall population was less than one-third of that in Richmond. An immoral, wicked place, indeed!

Among the horrific sights they witnessed at these houses of ill repute: intoxicated crowds of young men; dancing of a form that was "vile, vulgar, and degrading to the extreme"; and liquor sales. The latter of these provided a huge source of revenue for the madams. More intriguing than any of these sights, though, is the description of one more thing that the genteel ladies of the commission were exposed to:

> [T]he horrible practice of perversion, the most revolting and degrading of all vices, is permitted and encouraged in some of Lexington's houses. One madam declared that her inmates were all perverts, and boasted that her place was a favorite resort because of the practices performed by the inmates. The sickening details of these conditions are too awful to relate.

The mind boggles!

In addition to the sinful goings-on within the houses, there was the larger problem of how it affected the entire downtown district. The influx of women from other districts meant that increasing numbers of women were soliciting clients on the streets. One-third of Lexington's children lived within the Fourth Ward, where the vice district was located. These children were exposed to vice on a regular basis as they walked to and from school. The principal of the school within the vice district admitted that many of his female students would enter prostitution as soon as they turned fourteen.

How should the city deal with a problem so large that even the police offered recommendations to customers about which houses to visit? There was no question that prostitution was profitable to a great many people at all social levels. To ignore it would be to admit that the law had failed. Further, it was obvious that ignoring the problem would not make it go away. Segregation would have made the houses even easier to find, and it would not have solved the problem elsewhere in the city (a growing number of houses were springing up close to the university campus).

How also to deal with the public health risks arising from vice? Medical experts estimated that close to 50 percent of the nation's men suffered from gonorrhea. In turn, their wives and children would also face exposure. On a smaller but no less serious scale, syphilis was also a problem. Prostitution was marked as the source of these diseases. Regular medical inspections and certificates of clean health were an option. However, the commission feared that bills of health might only increase the temptation to vice. They would only be able to inspect those who registered as prostitutes, and so those with disease would not stop plying their trade; they would simply fail to register. The commission concluded, "There is no way to make promiscuous intercourse safe."

After careful consideration of the problem, and study of other cities and their methods of handling the problem of vice, the commission made a series of recommendations. The current laws were inadequate, with punishments so rarely handed out and fines so light that they failed to be a deterrent. Therefore, the recommendations addressed two levels. At the state level, suggestions included:

- creating a reformatory for the incarceration of prostitutes;
- a mandatory sentence of between one and five years in the reformatory for all prostitutes and madams;
- sentences in county jail or the workhouse for men caught patronizing prostitutes;
- allowing the circuit court to close down the houses and keep them locked for a period of one to three years.

At the city level, recommendations included:

- harsher penalties against prostitutes;
- changes to the existing vagrancy laws so that women without visible means of support (i.e., a husband or legitimate income) could be sent to the workhouse for thirty to fifty days;
- the closure of all parlor houses outside the vice district.

The report concluded with the overall suggestion that "all disorderly houses in the city of Lexington be closed immediately and kept closed entirely."

THE END OF MADAM BELLE

The city did not heed the call to close all houses of vice immediately. Real action did not come until army chiefs complained about the levels of vice and how it was contributing to the prevalence of sexually transmitted diseases among troops at nearby training camps. The First World War was in full swing, and the army did not need diseased men. At first the city's response was along the lines of, "Vice? What vice? We don't have that problem now." The army swiftly reminded city leaders of the Vice Commission's report. Most of the houses mentioned were still in business. If the sale of women and liquor continued, the training camps risked closure. Finally, the city listened.

By 1917, Belle Brezing could see the writing on the wall. The anti-vice and temperance movement was growing ever stronger. With an increasing fear of being arrested and sentenced to jail, and with the sense that the glory days were over, Belle made a decision. She called her girls to her one morning and announced that she was closing the business. She tearfully sent all of her girls away with enough money to start new lives. (Over the years, many had already gone on to prosperous futures as the wives or mistresses of wealthy men as far afield as California.) The carriages and horses were sold. A sign was posted outside the Megowan Street house declaring it a private residence.

Just like that, Belle Brezing's years as the most celebrated madam in America came to an end. Belle lived the rest of her years in relative seclusion. Her companion, Billy Mabon, had died of kidney disease in February 1917. Billy, once a member of Morgan's Raiders, had been Belle's lover and

This rare picture of Billy Mabon is thought to date from before he met Belle. *Courtesy of University of Kentucky.*

business representative for more than thirty years. Now she saw only her sister, Hester, her longtime cook and housekeeper, Pearl, and a few maids. She spent much of her time reading and battling her recurrent addiction to morphine. After Pearl and Hester both passed away in 1926, Belle's seclusion increased. The once elegant house fell into disrepair.

In 1938, she was diagnosed with uterine cancer. Ever mindful of the hospital's refusal of her donation so many years before, she insisted on staying in her own home, permitting only the doctor to visit her. On August 11, 1940, Belle Brezing passed away. As per her instructions, there was no visitation and no funeral. Notice of her death was not posted until she had been buried. A poem she had written appeared in the newspaper:

"Kisses"

Sitting to night in my chamber, a school girl figure
and lonely, I kiss the end of my finger, that and that only.
Reveries rises from the smokey mouth. Memories linger surround
me. Boys that are married or single. Gather around me. School boys
in pantalets romping, Boys that now are growing to be young lads,
Boys that liked to be Kissed; and like to give kisses.
Kisses. I remember them: Those in the corner were fleetest:
Sweet were those won the Sly in the Dark were the sweetest.
Girls are tender and gentle. To woo was almost to win them.
Their lips are good as ripe peaches, and cream for finger.
Girls are sometimes flirts, and coquettish; Now catch and Kiss if
you can sin: could I catch both—ah, wasent I a happy Girl.
Boys is pretty and blooming sweetly, yea sweetness over their rest!
Them I loved dearly and truely. Last and the best.

Belle is widely accepted to have been the inspiration for Madam Belle Watling in Margaret Mitchell's epic novel, *Gone with the Wind* (Mitchell's husband was an alumnus of the University of Kentucky and worked the local police beat for a newspaper). Although Mitchell always denied that Brezing was her inspiration, the similarities are remarkable, so much so that any Lexingtonian watching the movie upon its release recognized Madam Belle. Other than sharing the same name, both Brezing and Watling had a child who was sent away and rode around town in a fine black carriage. Both performed numerous charitable acts for the local community, including attempting to help fund local hospitals, but were turned away by the wealthier women in town. Even details of the house, including an orchestra and the fine furnishing, mirrored those of Belle Brezing.

Today, as one hundred years ago, Belle is both beloved and reviled by Lexington's citizens. To some, she is a whore who brought shame to the town. To others, she is a colorful addition to the town's history, remembered for her business acumen, as well as her generosity to those whom the "proper" members of society snubbed. A bed race in her honor is a part of the annual Best of the Bluegrass celebration.

Chapter 4
THE CHEATING CONGRESSMAN

Lest one think that salacious political scandals are a modern notion, and that the gentlemen of days gone by were far more respectable, I present the case of Congressman William Breckinridge. His story kept the newspapers busy with many a headline.

William Campbell Preston Breckinridge was born into one of Lexington's most prominent families. His grandfather, John Cabell Breckinridge, was elected to the Virginia legislature at the tender age of nineteen. John relocated in 1793 to Lexington, where he practiced law and created one of the state's finest horse breeding programs at Castleton Farm. He served as attorney general under President Thomas Jefferson.

John's son, Robert Jefferson Breckinridge, had a somewhat colorful youth, being expelled from Princeton for fighting and enjoying a life of drunken revelry after graduating from New York's Union College. Despite (or perhaps because of) his antics, he was elected to the Kentucky legislature. After the death of a child, however, he bid farewell to politics and his wild ways and joined the clergy, becoming a Presbyterian minister. For a decade, he was pastor at a church in Baltimore, Maryland, and then he served a brief tenure as president of Pennsylvania's Jefferson College before returning to Lexington, where he pastored at a local church. As state supervisor of public education, he is credited with increasing school attendance tenfold within Kentucky. He then took a position as a professor of theology at the seminary in Danville. During the Civil War, his support of Abraham Lincoln put him at odds with some in his family; as was the case with many a Kentucky family, two of his sons fought for the Union and two for the Confederacy.

Among Robert's sons were Robert Jefferson Breckinridge Jr., a Confederate colonel and judge, and Joseph Cabell Breckinridge Sr., a Union soldier, promoted to major general during the Spanish-American War and inspector general of the army.

Then there was William. Born in Baltimore in 1837, William Campbell Preston Breckinridge seemed certain to follow in his family's illustrious footsteps. After graduating from Louisville's Law School in 1857, he began a law career in Lexington. Two years later, he married Lucretia Clay, granddaughter of statesman Henry Clay. Sadly, she died just thirteen months into their marriage. The child they had died shortly thereafter. In 1861, William remarried, taking as his wife Issa Desha, granddaughter of a former Kentucky governor. The couple would have seven children together.

W.C.P. Breckinridge. The dashing young politician may have advised chastity, but he didn't practice what he preached.

When war broke out between the states, he joined the Confederate army, where he was eventually appointed a colonel in the Ninth Kentucky Cavalry. His military career was a distinguished one, and he provided personal guard to Confederate president Jefferson Davis in the final few months before surrender. Upon return to Lexington, he took over as editor of the *Observer and Reporter* and dedicated himself to building a successful law practice. His reputation as an accomplished attorney spread, and in 1875 William entered into a professional partnership with another prominent lawyer, John Shelby.

POLITICAL CAREER

In 1869, William Breckinridge sought local political office. He ran for the position of county attorney but was defeated; his support of allowing blacks to testify in courts was considered far too progressive for the era. Undeterred, William spent the next decade developing his reputation as a skilled orator. Many of his contemporaries claimed that he was unequalled by any other Kentuckian of the day in his talent for capturing a jury with his excellent speaking abilities.

In 1884, Breckinridge was elected to the U.S. House of Representatives. One of his election platforms was the promotion of chastity, and he frequently counseled young women that "chastity is the foundation, the corner-stone of human society." He served five terms as a congressman and was recognized as one of the Democratic Party's greatest advocates for free trade and individual rights.

It seemed as if his career could only climb to greater heights—but then scandal broke. For all of his promotion of chastity and morality, William Breckinridge liked the ladies. Some say his tastes for women of all races and social backgrounds were a well-known secret and that he was on a first-name basis with some of Lexington's madams. His liking for one lady in particular would be his undoing.

MISS MADELINE POLLARD

Madeline Valeria Pollard was born in Frankfort, Kentucky, in 1866. Depending on which and whose history you read, her father was alternately described as a small-town lawyer, a teacher or a carpenter. Whatever the case, he apparently encouraged education in all of his children. After his death in 1876, Madeline was sent to reside with an aunt in Pittsburgh; there she studied music and attended school with her cousins. After a while, homesickness set in, and the young girl returned to Kentucky, living with a maternal aunt just outside Lexington. She had few friends or acquaintances, other than relatives, but longed to further her studies.

In time, a young gentleman, James Rodes, proposed to her. On her mother's advice, Madeline came to some written agreement with him that he would loan her money to pursue schooling. Presumably, it was his hope that in doing so, she would learn to appreciate and love him enough to accept his marriage proposal. (It should be noted that her mother would later deny any knowledge of Madeline's engagement.) The details of this agreement are somewhat vague, but it appears that for a time, she entered a convent, all the while concealing her engagement. She then attended Wesleyan College, with Mr. Rodes as her guardian. In 1884, or thereabouts, she transferred from Wesleyan to Lexington's Sayre School, an esteemed girls school that had been established some thirty years earlier.

The Sayre School was established in 1854 as a women's college. Today the school operates as a coed K-12 facility. *Courtesy of Lexington History Museum.*

During her time as a student at Sayre School, she met William C.P. Breckinridge. Although still married to Issa, Colonel Breckinridge had something of a reputation as a ladies man. When he went to speak to the young ladies at Sayre, no doubt the tall, famous man appeared quite dashing—the distinguished war hero, resplendent as he spoke to them of the virtues of womanhood. It is possible that this was not the first time that Madeline had met the congressman. Later, both would describe how they had met on a train from Cincinnati, each saying that the other had approached them. She would eventually claim that it was he who arranged for her to leave Wesleyan and enroll at Sayre.

After she completed her education, Breckinridge used his political contacts to help secure a position for Madeline within a government department, but she apparently was dismissed after making a disparaging remark about General Sherman at the time of his death. The two were not seen in public together, nor was there any reason to suspect that anything untoward might be taking place, but after the death of Mrs. Breckinridge in 1892, there were multiple rumors that Colonel Breckinridge and Miss Pollard were engaged to be married. Madeline was more than happy to substantiate the rumors. Meanwhile, friends of the congressman claimed that he consistently denied their truthfulness.

BREACH OF PROMISE

Madeline's hopes of becoming the third Mrs. Breckinridge crumbled when, in July 1893, William publicly announced that he had taken a new wife: Mrs. Louisa Scott Wing, the widow of a minister. They say that hell hath no fury like a woman scorned. The fury of Madeline Pollard would soon destroy both the career and reputation of Colonel William Breckinridge.

"A Congressman in Trouble" was the headline that broke the news on August 13, 1893. Madeline Valeria Pollard had filed suit against Breckinridge in the Supreme Court of the District of Columbia, seeking the sum of $50,000 for breach of promise. In her suit, Madeline claimed that she had met the congressman on a train from Cincinnati in 1883 and that he later came to visit her at Wesleyan Seminary. He then used his smooth-talking ways and manly wiles to take advantage of her. Perhaps

"Skeleton Will Out." The cartoon is from a series illustrating the Breckinridge-Pollard affair.

the most shocking news of all was that she had allegedly given birth to two children, of whom one had died and one was given up for adoption. She claimed that he proposed marriage on several occasions and that she saw no reason not to believe his intentions, until she heard that he had married Mrs. Wing.

This was the type of story that, then as now, had tongues wagging and journalists scrambling to outdo one another with the biggest scoop. The newspapers reported that, upon learning of the lawsuit, William Breckinridge seemed surprisingly unperturbed. Perhaps he did not think that Miss Pollard's story would carry weight. Or perhaps, as his later behavior would indicate, he believed himself to be so highly regarded and so prominent that no scandal could tarnish his reputation.

THE COURT HEARINGS

Testimony in the case of *Pollard v. Breckinridge* was heard in the spring of 1894. The case caught the attention of the nation. During the next month or so, events outside the courtroom often proved as interesting as those within: Breckinridge's son, Desha, was a member of his legal team. (You will remember Desha from the first chapter for his quick temper and desire to duel.) Desha's outbursts of temper led to several violent altercations with members of opposing counsel, one of which required the bailiffs to intervene and physically drag him from the courtroom.

Colonel Breckinridge refused to discuss the trial with the press, but several friends were quick to defend him. They remarked that no man could be expected to marry a woman of such unchaste character as Miss Pollard. Further, they claimed to have found a witness who would testify to having gone through a mock marriage ceremony with the young lady in question. Other claims against her character involved several alleged lovers and a dispute about her age. A doctor in Danville testified that the now deceased Colonel Swope (of the Swope-Goodloe tragedy) had brought Miss Pollard to him for an "illegal procedure" (presumably an abortion). He further swore that Swope had claimed responsibility for her condition.

Among the other depositions taken was that of Mrs. Julia Blackburn, widow of former Kentucky governor Luke Blackburn. Mrs. Blackburn testified that Colonel Breckinridge had brought Miss Pollard to her so that they could become better acquainted. She had acted as chaperone and introduced the young woman to the Washington social circle. Upon hearing of his marriage to Mrs. Wing, the widow Blackburn had expressed her surprise to the congressman, to which he apparently replied that his children would not hear of him entering a marriage with someone so young as Miss Pollard. Interestingly, when rumors of his marriage to Mrs. Wing first became public, Breckinridge's response had been that the rumors were absurd but that he was happy for them to spread because it might accustom his children to the idea that he would one day remarry.

Mrs. Blackburn later testified in court on behalf of Madeline. Speaking to a crowded courtroom, she claimed that she had been present when Colonel Breckinridge proposed marriage to Madeline, stating that he expressed a need to wait until an appropriate amount of time had passed since the death of his second wife before they could make a public announcement. At the same time, he repeatedly denied to Mrs. Blackburn and to Miss Pollard that there was any relationship with Mrs. Wing. The police superintendent of Washington and a local doctor likewise testified that Breckinridge had presented Madeline to them and declared their intent to marry. These were three well-respected members of the community, all of whom held a certain amount of weight with the court. Among other witnesses on her behalf was a midwife who testified that she had delivered the second child and that Colonel Breckinridge had paid the resulting medical bills.

Sarah Gess, a former slave who owned a "house of assignation," gave testimony regarding the meetings between the couple at her home. Kentucky law did not allow her to testify in the state so she traveled to Washington. Gess had known Breckinridge for many years when he came to her asking that she provide a room for Madeline one weekend so that they might meet in private. He stayed until late each night, kissed her "very affectionately" and paid the bill. The madam further testified that the bed was clearly rumpled after each of his visits. Their meetings at her house totaled more than fifty, and Madeline never visited at any other time. When news of the court case broke, Breckinridge contacted Sarah, asking that she not mention his visits. Sarah refused, telling him that he should not have misled the young woman. The owner of a Washington boardinghouse gave similar testimony about regular visits from Colonel Breckinridge while Miss Pollard was staying with her.

On March 16, Madeline took the stand to state her case. With no money of her own, she was living at the Episcopal House of Mercy. Thanks to the assistance of Mrs. Blackburn, who had rallied her friends, money had been raised to pay her legal bills. Arriving at the court each day, dressed in black and with a nun as her companion, she presented herself as a model of proper Southern womanhood. In a small voice, Madeline told the court of how the congressman had approached her on the train, using that old line that has worked so well for generations: "Don't I know you from somewhere?" When he asked if he might call on her, she replied that he was welcome to call on her mother and ask permission. Choosing to skip the expected protocol of meeting the parents, Breckinridge had taken her to a disreputable house of assignation shortly after he had met.

Once there, he attempted to seduce her. At first, she resisted, as any proper lady would do, but then she gave in to his "most wonderful power of persuasion." Upon his recommendation and with his assistance, Madeline transferred from Wesleyan to Lexington's Sayre School, and whilst there, they continued their secret relationship. He accompanied her to concerts and other summer events, telling the teachers at Sayre that he was her chaperone, an old friend of her father. In 1884, she became pregnant; Breckinridge spirited her away to an Ohio asylum, where the child was born the following year. She admitted that he fathered another child, who was born in 1888 at an orphan asylum but died a few months later. Breckinridge had told her that she must give up both children, lest they be traced back to him. He paid all medical and funeral expenses.

After the death of his second wife, Madeline had reason to believe that they could now be together as a couple. She depicted a romantic scene from August 1892, in which Colonel Breckinridge met her from the train, swept her into his arms and kissed her. Now that his children were grown, he proclaimed, there was no reason they could not be married. She accepted his proposal, and they spent several days together in Washington discussing marriage plans. They then went to New York together. Although he wanted to wait one year from the death of his wife before remarrying, she suggested that two years would be a proper time to wait, to give the children time to grieve and to accept the idea of a new wife. During that time, she would travel to Europe to study at a young ladies' school in Berlin. When she returned, they would marry. She turned down the scholarship to Berlin after Breckinridge begged her to, arguing that he could not bear for her to be away that long.

A third pregnancy came to light in 1893, but according to Miss Pollard, Breckinridge decided that he would acknowledge this one since they would be married by the time the child was born. She claims that they even spent time discussing names. But then he requested that they postpone their marriage until after the child's birth so that he would not be known as the father. When the unexpected news of his marriage to Mrs. Wing was made known, Madeline suffered a miscarriage from the shock.

What then, the attorneys asked, of her engagement to James Rodes? Madeline denied having ever accepted his proposal of marriage. Instead, she claimed, he had promised to pay for her education, and she in return would either marry him or pay him back his expenses with interest. She stated that her mother had drawn up an agreement between the two. Perhaps conveniently, the location of the agreement was unknown. Miss Pollard suggested that it might be in Breckinridge's possession. As for his letters, she had never kept them since she did not hold them dear as one might those from a fiancé. Finally, Rodes had written, demanding that she marry him or pay him back immediately. Writing to Colonel Breckinridge for advice, he came to see her in person at Wesleyan. She produced numerous letters and telegrams from the congressman as evidence of their relationship, which had even continued one month after his marriage to Mrs. Wing.

Next came the testimony on behalf of Congressman Breckinridge. As was to be expected, the defense's case relied heavily on besmirching the character of Miss Pollard. Several depositions were presented as evidence that Breckinridge had been elsewhere on the dates Madeline claimed they had been together. Some of these claims were rather tenuous—for example, those arguing that he was present at trials in Versailles and Nicholasville. With Lexington being such a short distance away, the congressman could still have made the journey for nightly trysts.

Several men came forth claiming to be formerly engaged to the young lady in question. A Lexington carpenter, appropriately named William

"Colonel Breckinridge on the Witness Stand."

Wood, claimed that she had broken off their engagement when he revealed that he could not afford to take her to Europe. The Nicholasville School superintendent, Ranklin Rosell, testified that he had been engaged to Madeline while she attended Wesleyan and he was a clerk working in Cincinnati. He apparently broke off their engagement for a somewhat odd reason (by today's standards): "I didn't like the freedom with which she allowed me to kiss her. It was not the way I wished to love the woman I wanted to marry and to be loved by her."

One wonders why he had not made the engagement public at the time. A more cynical mind might also speculate whether monetary and political influence from a U.S. congressman had helped him attain his current position. Depositions from a Lexington butcher and the chief of police further served to damage Miss Pollard's character. Both claimed that they had met her at a "questionable house" and that she had claimed to be three years older than she now pretended to be. Mrs. William Miller testified that she and Madeline had both lived at the same "questionable house."

Another, more bizarre, story was that of Aleck Julian, a blind man who claimed that he had undergone a mock marriage ceremony with Miss Pollard in 1882 and that she, being in a drunken state, had then kissed him. Although he went on to testify that she was a most modest girl and that they never engaged in anything more intimate, the goal of the defense was to indicate that she was far from the naïve creature she claimed to be. With so many reputed marriages, engagements and secret relationships, she must have clearly been a busy woman.

Although friends of the congressman had previously claimed that he would not testify on his own behalf, it seems the silver-tongued orator could not remain silent when the spotlight shone so heavily on him. In a scene that no doubt mirrored more recent Washington political scandals, Breckinridge strongly denied that he had ever made love to Miss Pollard. He had met her on a train, when she introduced herself to him as Madeline Breckinridge Pollard, on her way to visit her sister, who was dying. He offered his sympathies and thought nothing more of the meeting until she wrote requesting that he visit her in Cincinnati regarding an important matter. Breckinridge replied that such a journey would be inconvenient but that she would be most welcome to call on him when she was next in Lexington.

They did later meet in Cincinnati, and Miss Pollard told him of her situation with Rodes, claiming that a forced marriage was imminent. Tearfully, she declared that she could not marry Rodes because "I know what other men are and his very presence is offensive to me." He advised her to marry Rodes and returned to Lexington the next day.

During his second day on the stand, Breckinridge repeatedly emphasized that he had never proposed marriage, given that she was not chaste when he met her, nor had he fathered any children with Miss Pollard. Rather than a naïve young girl of seventeen, he claimed that she was, in fact, a young woman of twenty-one "with nothing to indicate that she was not experienced in the relations of sexes." He painted her as a skilled temptress who used her feminine wiles to ensnare him. For his part, he was but a weak-willed man: "I was a man of passion. She was a woman of passion. There was no seduction, no seduction on either side. It was simply a case of human passion."

Finally, testimony was complete. In his closing remarks, Pollard's attorneys declared that the idea of an experienced man such as Colonel

"Madeline Gets a Verdict."

Breckinridge being the victim in this case would be laughable were it not such a serious case. The jury agreed. After little more than an hour of deliberations, they ruled in favor of Madeline Pollard and awarded her $15,000 in damages. Although Madeline was not present in the court for the jury's decision (despite illustrations depicting a jubilant young woman raising her hands in thanks to the heavens), witnesses said that Breckinridge turned pale at the announcement. He immediately demanded a retrial and launched an appeal, but the judge denied all motions and ruled the jury's verdict final.

SEEKS REELECTION

Breckinridge's reputation was in tatters. His chapter of the Freemasons dismissed him. His church membership had been threatened; he had confessed to the church leaders, and for a while there were some question as to whether he would be expelled. They did decide to accept his request for forgiveness and readmitted him. Even so, surely his political career was over.

William Breckinridge did not believe so. Whether through confidence or arrogance, the congressman firmly believed that the Pollard trial and the publicity it generated would have no adverse bearing on his ability to be reelected. Even before the trial was complete, he announced his intentions to continue his political career. In May 1894, he told journalists, "I feel a renewed confidence that I will be returned to the House…They have nothing more that they can shoot at me."

However, he had not counted on the influence of the angry wives of Lexington. Women may not have been able to vote, but they knew that they could wield considerable clout over their husbands. They had little time for a man who had been revealed as a cheat and a womanizing scoundrel. With the trial ongoing, a group of influential women in the city gathered to call for his impeachment. Among the signees were the wives of Cassius Clay and William Cassius Goodloe, as well as several women from family of his first wife, Lucretia Clay. A few weeks later, Washington, D.C., members of the Woman's Suffrage Association and the Women's Christian Temperance Union united to express their disapproval of the male-female double standard and to call for the resignation of Colonel Breckinridge. They went on to form the Women's Protective League, with the aims of securing equal rights and protecting "women who have been wronged."

While Breckinridge rallied his supporters, the women of Lexington campaigned against him, working tirelessly in their neighborhoods and their churches and organizing boycotts of businesses known to donate to the congressman's campaign. Nor did they focus entirely on their economic power. A gentleman whose father contributed to Breckinridge's campaign might find his dinner engagement with a young woman canceled. A husband might find himself unwelcome in the bedroom. These women knew that they wielded another source of power.

Their efforts paid off. In September 1894, Breckinridge narrowly lost his nomination to William Claiborne Owens of Georgetown. He tried to contest the results but eventually had no choice but to admit defeat. Son Desha's fiery temper revealed itself again after the results were announced. Earlier the same day, he had to be dragged away from a local judge when he tried to attack him. Later in the day, James Livingstone, a member of the Owens campaign, moved to shake hands after the election, but the younger Breckinridge refused, declaring, "You are a one-horse scoundrel, and I will not take your hand." He went on to call Livingstone a liar, at which point the man responded by delivering a punch in Desha Breckinridge's face. A peaceable man may have walked away, but the provoker of this argument was no such man. Desha chose to stab Livingstone, causing serious injury although fortunately missing his original target, the heart. He then kicked the wounded man (some newspapers claimed that this indicated a desire for no more bloodshed) until onlookers dragged him away. No charges appear to have been filed against the yielder of the knife, and James Livingstone later moved to New York.

One final fascinating postscript to Breckinridge's career took place in February 1895. Although he had lost the nomination, Breckinridge was finishing out his term of office. During a Congressional hearing about Hawaii, he was angered to find that discussion was cut short and the focus moved to another topic. The Kentucky congressman was passing by John Taddeus Heard, a Democrat from Missouri, when he suddenly turned on the man, calling him a liar and a scoundrel. Breckinridge then attempted to hit Mr. Heard, but two other members of the house jumped into the fray and restrained him. With Congress in an uproar, the Speaker had to call

W.C.P. Breckinridge in his later years. *Courtesy of University of Louisville, Law Library Collection.*

on the sergeant at arms to bring order, which he did by arresting Colonel Breckinridge. Both he and Mr. Heard were led away for questioning. The two men eventually returned to the floor and offered their apologies.

Once his political career was over, Breckinridge returned to Lexington and worked at the newspaper overseen by his son Desha. A later attempt to reenter politics failed. Colonel William Breckinridge died in his sleep in 1904.

And what of Miss Pollard? Despite receiving many offers from theatrical agents, inviting her to go on stage, Madeline moved to London, England, where she reportedly spent several years studying. After that, she appears to have faded into obscurity. The fate of the child given away for adoption is not known.

Chapter 5

TO BE BLACK IN LEXINGTON

On January 18, 1878, a story in the *New York Times* drew a simple but effective contrast. Grove Kennedy, part of an infamous family of (white) outlaws, saw his murder conviction overturned by the Kentucky Court of Appeals, despite being known to have killed at least six men. Meanwhile, three black men in Lexington were killed by an angry mob. Their crime? Possibly having knowledge about the murder of a white man. The murderer had immediately been hanged for the crime, but two weeks later a mob arrived at the home of Tom Turner. When he refused to leave his house, the mob shot him dead as his wife watched helplessly. Two other men, Edward Claxton and John Davis, were dragged from their homes and hanged from a nearby tree. The implication of the story was clear: this was yet another example of so-called Kentucky justice, a justice sullied by racism.

SLAVERY

The area known as Cheapside, next to the former courthouse in downtown Lexington, is now favored for its bars, restaurants and a pedestrian patio where live music entertains diners during the summer months. Its history is less joyful. In the 1840s and 1850s, Lexington was home to one of the largest slave markets in the South, second only to New Orleans. Cheapside was where buyers from

Cheapside at the turn of the twentieth century. *Courtesy of Patti and Chuck Starr.*

across the country would gather to buy their slaves. One former slave recalls: "The slave traders would…take them to Lexington where they owned a trading yard and put them in there and feed them well before the slave trader came from New Orleans to buy them, just the same as horse purchasers."

The good food would last just enough to ensure that the merchandise looked fit and healthy at the time of sale. Slaves would be auctioned off to the highest bidder at a special sale block that stood for many years in the center of Cheapside—a dark reminder of the past. On another corner stood the whipping post, used for public punishment of slaves who had committed such offenses as being out in the evening. One woman remembered the day her sister and father were sold (taken from the *Born in Slavery* collection): "[She] was only twelve years of age when sold, and her master received $1,220 for her, then she was taken south to some plantation…There was a long line of slaves to be sold and after they were sold and a good price paid for each they were handcuffed and marched away to the South." She would never see them again.

Collections of slave narratives shed some light on life as a slave in Kentucky. Uncle Wes Woods, once a slave in Monroe County, told an interviewer for the Federal Writers' Project in the 1930s: "Some slaves were treated good, and some were treated awful bad by the white people; but most of them were treated good if they would do what their master told them to do." Nevertheless, his very next sentence tells of a girl who was tied to the rafters of a barn and whipped so badly that "blood ran down her back and made a large pool on the ground."

Slave quarters at Rose Hill. *Courtesy of Library of Congress.*

Although it was not illegal for slaves to read in Kentucky, the majority of slaves in the state were not allowed access to books, and "if found looking at a book, a slave was whipped unmercifully." Very few owners allowed them to marry. Carl Hall, a slave in Boyd County, remembers that "any attempt to mate with a negro woman brought swift, sure horrible punishment, and the species were propogated [*sic*] by selected male negroes who were kept for that purpose. The owners of this privileged negro charged a fee of one out of every four of his offspring for his services." Much like the horse breeders of the Bluegrass loan out the prized stallion for breeding, so did slave owners breed their stock to ensure strength and hardiness.

Slaves made up about half of the population in Lexington and Fayette County. Unlike in rural areas, slaves in the city were much more visible and were permitted a certain amount of freedom (albeit still within the realms of slavery) to come and go to the market, blacksmith and so on, as their daily tasks required. Often, a master might not have much use for his slaves around the house, and so he would hire them out to local employers. Some

$150 REWARD.

R ANAWAY from the subscriber, on the night of Monday the 11th July, a negro man named

TOM,

about 30 years of age, 5 feet 6 or 7 inches high; of dark color; heavy in the chest; several of his jaw teeth out; and upon his body are several old marks of the whip, one of them straight down the back. He took with him a quantity of clothing, and several hats.

A reward of $150 will be paid for his apprehension and security, if taken out of the State of Kentucky; $100 if taken in any county bordering on the Ohio river; $50 if taken in any of the interior counties except Fayette; or $20 if taken in the latter county.
july 12-84-tf   B. L. BOSTON.

Left: A notice offering a reward for the capture of a runaway slave who has obviously been beaten.

Below: Slave quarters in Bourbon County. *Courtesy of Library of Congress.*

would head to work in the factories and on the railroad, others might be seen digging sewers and working in the downtown taverns. Former slave Milton Clarke commented on the fate of some who were sent to work in the Lexington hemp-bagging factories:

An overseer of one of these factories, Tom Monks, would tie up his poor boys, and give them from forty to fifty hashes. He kept them sometimes yoked with iron collars, with prongs sticking out, and the name of the owner written on them. Working in these factories takes all the life and spirit out of a young slave, and he soon becomes little better than an idiot. This is the worst kind of slavery in Kentucky. When the life is thus taken out of these poor lads, at the age of eighteen or twenty, they are sold for Louisiana.

Others fared better and were able to experience at least a small pretense of freedom. After a while, concern grew that such freedom might create among slaves a sense of independence, a lack of respect. As fears grew, policing went into effect. Blacks were required to carry papers from their owners indicating that they had permission to be outdoors unaccompanied. A curfew was put in place to ensure that they did not wander around in the evenings.

LEWIS C. ROBARDS

One name was synonymous with the cruelty and abhorrent nature of the slave trade in Kentucky: Lewis C. Robards. From his pens on West Short Street, Robards made his fortune selling slaves, be they obtained legally or otherwise. Any black who happened in his path might be considered fair game, and he cared not whether they were free or enslaved, healthy or sick.

Attitudes toward the slave trader were best summed up by the words of Abraham Lincoln. In an 1854 speech, he said: "You have among you a sneaking individual of the class of native tyrants, known as the 'slave dealer.' You despise him utterly…If you are obliged to deal with him, you try to get through the job without so much as touching him."

One of Robards's favorite methods of building business was to send slave-stealers (or agents) into eastern Kentucky, where they would kidnap free black men, women and children. With only their word that they were free (and any paperwork to back their claims having been destroyed), the unfortunate abductees were sold back into slavery, often being sent downriver to New Orleans, where there was less chance that anyone would recognize them. In a similar vein, if a slave was stopped in Lexington and did not have papers

The Robards Slave Jail was demolished after the Civil War, and an African American church was built on the site. *From the collection of Barton K. Bataille.*

granting him permission from his owner to be there, he might be sent back to his master, or a less scrupulous man might simply sell him for a profit. Being shipped south held other implications for those sold into slavery. In Kentucky, slave life typically meant being either a household slave or working on a farm. Conditions were much harsher on the plantations and cotton fields of Louisiana and Mississippi; families were ripped apart, severe punishments were commonplace and one's life expectancy was quite diminished.

On a few occasions, kidnap victims were rescued before being sold. Children snatched in other states were found in Robards's pens. Sadly, though, such instances were rare. One notable instance of an attempt to help slaves to their freedom occurred in 1848. A student at Danville's Centre College, E.J. Doyle (who went by the name of Patrick), took a group of about seventy-five slaves, some of the finest in Fayette County. They crept away in the dead of night and had nearly reached the Ohio River—and freedom—when a posse of several hundred men caught up with them. Fighting ensued, and Doyle was

Right: This runaway slave notice offers a reward before he reaches the Kentucky-Ohio border—and freedom.

Below: Some slaves enjoyed much more freedom in Kentucky than they would have had in the Deep South, but others were still subjected to vicious beatings.

$150 REWARD

RANAWAY from the subscriber, on the night of the 2d instant, a negro man, who calls himself *Henry May*, about 22 years old, 5 feet 6 or 8 inches high, ordinary color, rather chunky built, bushy head, and has it divided mostly on one side, and keeps it very nicely combed; has been raised in the house, and is a first rate dining-room servant, and was in a tavern in Louisville for 18 months. I expect he is now in Louisville trying to make his escape to a free state, (in all probability to Cincinnati, Ohio.) Perhaps he may try to get employment on a steamboat. He is a good cook, and is handy in any capacity as a house servant. Had on when he left, a dark cassinett coatee, and dark striped cassinett pantaloons, new—he had other clothing. I will give $50 reward if taken in Louisvill; 100 dollars if taken one hundred miles from Louisville in this State, and 150 dollars if taken out of this State, and delivered to me, or secured in any jail so that I can get him again. WILLIAM BURKE.

Bardstown, Ky., September 3d, 1838.

brought back to Lexington, where he received a sentence of twenty years hard labor. Three black ringleaders were hanged, while most of the others were sold down the river. Were any able to make it to freedom in the confusion of the fighting? We shall never know.

Business dealing in slaves was brisk in the 1840s, and soon Robards bought more property to house his "merchandise." In 1851, he bought what had formerly been the Lexington Theatre. Here, he kept his "fancy girls"—lighter-skinned women whom he would sell to serve as mistresses. In contrast to the filthy, straw-lined pens where the other slaves were kept, these girls stayed in nicely furnished apartments. Robards would entertain prospective buyers before escorting them upstairs, where they could inspect the girls with "intimate examinations." The price for one of his "fancy girls"? Between $1,000 and $2,000 ($35,000 to $48,000 in today's market). A regular female slave might sell for about $500, while a skilled male slave (for example, a blacksmith) might fetch as much as $3,000.

The public sales of Robards's "fancy girls" seems particularly repugnant to read about today. Abolitionist minister Calvin Fairbank recalled in his memoir one particular sale that took place in Lexington in 1843. Eliza was "one of the most beautiful and exquisite young girls one could expect to find in freedom or slavery." The daughter of a slave owner, she was, in fact, only sixty-fourth black and had been confined to Robards's upper rooms before her sale. Fairbank rushed to Cincinnati to meet with fellow abolitionists and secured money to buy her. On the day of the sale, he estimated that there were some two thousand people present, from as far afield as Boston and New Orleans. His disgust at the sale is evident in his writing:

> *Upon the block…stood the auctioneer by his victim…the embodiment of Diabolus, trained and anxious for his work. He directed attention to the valuable piece of property…calling particular attention to her exquisite qualities as a mistress for any gentleman. And this he kept prominent, in the most insinuating and vile manner, outraging common decency.*

Bidding began. Soon only Fairbank and a Frenchman from New Orleans remained in the bidding war. At one point, the Frenchman turned to the minister, asking, "How high will you bid, Monsieur."

The reply: "Higher than you."

Undeterred by the competition, the Frenchman shrugged and bid again. Each time, Calvin Fairbank bid higher still, until he was offering $1,450. His opponent wavered, and for a brief moment the auctioneer looked set to use his hammer. Suddenly, he had a better idea. Before the crowd, he ripped open Eliza's dress, revealing her naked breasts to the crowd in an attempt to entice the men to a higher price:

A suppressed cry of shame, and contempt—of anger and grief—a bitter murmur of Kentucky wrath and disgust, rolled like a wave through that throng. Southern women blushed, and Mr. Wickliffe hung his head for shame; and such exclamations as "Too bad!" "What a shame!" "Horrible!" could be heard on every side, from both North and South.

Bidding rose to $1,475.

Again the Frenchman asked Fairbank, "How high do you intend to go?"

"It is none of your business, sir; but understand that you cannot command enough money to take this girl."

Not content with the price on offer, the auctioneer continued his public humiliation of the poor woman, this time lifting her skirt to her waist and slapping her exposed behind. As members of the crowd wept, the Frenchman made one final bid. Before the hammer could declare Eliza sold, Calvin Fairbank threw out a higher price.

"Sold!"

As the auctioneer grumbled about the low price, he asked the girl's new owner what he planned to do with her. There could only be one answer.

"Free her, sir!"

Amid a cheering crowd, Fairbank took her to her aunt's house while papers declaring her freedom were drawn up. A few days after, Eliza traveled to Cincinnati, where other abolitionists helped her to complete her education. She later married, and "for forty-three years filled a position of honor…and none but her husband and a few chosen friends know that she was ever a slave, or that she has a drop of African blood in her veins."

Sadly, this tale is but one amid thousands of others that ended in wretched misery for those on the auction block. One also wonders if the urge to free her would have been so strong had Eliza held a greater amount of African blood. Was it the auctioneer's actions that so shamed the crowd that day? Or was it that he was doing it to a woman who, to the average passerby, looked white? Fairbank went on to serve several prison sentences for helping slaves to escape. In 1851, he was sent to the state penitentiary for fifteen years.

Robards's success as one of the leading slave traders also led to his downfall. His proclivity for going to any length to make a sale, even if that meant lying about the health of the person being sold, led to numerous lawsuits from dissatisfied buyers. Soon the debts from those lawsuits began to mount. Lewis C. Robards was forced to sell his business to help pay his bills. A slave dealer named R.S. Thompson purchased the pens. Within a few years, the Civil War broke out, and the buildings were used as a military prison until fire destroyed the jail in 1864.

In a beautiful example of poetic justice, an African American church was constructed on the site of a former Robards property in the 1890s. The dedication of the First Congregational Church recorded that it had been "built by a people no longer in bondage." The church is still standing today. A key that may have once opened the slave pens is reportedly still in their care.

THE CIVIL WAR

Kentucky suffered greatly between 1861 and 1865. It was one of the few states to be truly split. After all, the presidents of both the Union and the Confederacy were born in the commonwealth—Abraham Lincoln in Hodgenville and Jefferson Davis in Pembroke. The tobacco fields and farming estates relied on slave labor, while slavery was far less common in the mountainous regions of the east.

Kentucky never seceded from the Union; in 1861, Governor Beriah Magoffin and the legislature declared the state neutral. Nevertheless, the state was a strategic point on the route between north and south. Within the first year of war, the Confederacy claimed Columbus, while Union troops moved into Paducah and Louisville. Soon, families and communities were divided as brother fought against brother, father against son, neighbor against neighbor. In Lexington, houses at opposite sides of Gratz Park served as headquarters for opposing sides of troops, while some buildings served alternately as both Confederate and Union hospitals. Many historians have suggested that the majority of Kentuckians may have supported the Union at the start of the war, but by the end, "a clear majority had assumed a decidedly Confederate identity." Part of the reason for this was a resistance to government interference in state rights, including slavery.

Once the Civil War was over and Reconstruction got underway, Kentucky seemed to embrace racial violence. George C. Wright, author of *Racial Violence in Kentucky, 1865–1940*, noted, "White Kentuckians responded to the social, political, and other changes with unheard of violence, even by

Kentucky standards." Emancipation removed the only protection (albeit tenuous and inhumane) that blacks in Kentucky had—being the property of someone. The Kentucky legal system offered no protection for newly freed African Americans and often upheld white violence by refusing to punish white-on-black crime. In rural areas of the state, the Ku Klux Klan waged a campaign of terror, as described in this memory from *Recollections of Mary*, a former slave: "De Klu Klux uster stick de niggers head on er stake alongside de road…and dar de buzzards would eat them till nuthin' was left but de bones. Dar war a sign on dis stake dat said 'Look out Nigger You are next.'"

So what of Lexington during the Reconstruction? The black population of the city increased as former slaves from rural areas sought the protection of black communities within the larger cities. Others fled the state in hope of finding security up north. The influx of new lower-income residents led to a demand for more housing. Cheap neighborhoods of shotgun shacks sprang up in parts of the city. Typically named for the landowner or developer, these housing areas were in the less desirable areas, near stockyards or next to railroads. Lexington was not segregated, with poor black neighborhoods and wealthier white ones.

Those who stayed faced little assistance in creating new lives for themselves. Neither local nor state courts would consider testimony by blacks against whites. The only potential avenue for recourse was the Freedmen's Bureau.

"Freedmen's Bureau Giving Rations to Old and Sick." *Courtesy of Library of Congress.*

The Freedmen's Bureau was the only source of legal assistance for former slaves in Kentucky, but many bureau officers fled the state in fear for their lives. *Courtesy of Library of Congress.*

Established in 1865 by President Lincoln, the Bureau of Refugees, Freedmen and Abandoned Land (or Freedmen's Bureau) aimed to assist former slaves during the Reconstruction process—helping them to find work, housing, education and healthcare. Always envisioned as a temporary agency, it was eventually disbanded in 1869 by President Grant. During the four years of its existence, the bureau found itself becoming a de facto legal system for many freed slaves, particularly in areas where courts refused to acknowledge the rights granted by the Thirteenth and Fourteenth Amendments. In Kentucky, where former slaves made up one-fifth of the population, agents served as advocates for freed blacks, helping to reunite families and levying fines against whites when they refused to honor contracts. They came up against heavy resistance; many whites did not accept emancipation. J. Michael Rhyne noted that "many white men and women in Kentucky, including some Bureau agents…simply did not believe in black equality." The commonwealth would not ratify the Thirteenth or Fourteenth Amendment until March 18, 1976.

JOHN BUSH V. KENTUCKY

The question of jury fairness went as far as the U.S. Supreme Court with the 1879 death of Annie van Meter and the subsequent trial of John Bush.

In 1878, prominent local businessman Joseph van Meter, hired John Bush and his wife, Mary, both former slaves, to work as servants within his household. In January of the following year, the events of one tragic evening left seventeen-year-old daughter Annie dead from a bullet wound. John claimed that his employer had returned home drunk and accused his servant of spreading rumors about Mrs. Van Meter. He attempted to shoot John but, in his intoxicated state, missed and instead shot his daughter. Van Meter claimed that his daughter had been attempting to end a romantic relationship with Bush and that the rejected man had shot her in a fit of rage. Given the era and place, it was not surprising that the police should believe the white man. John Bush was promptly arrested and charged with murder.

But then something unexpected happened. The local black community, believing that John was the victim of an unfair legal system and suspecting that he had been framed, rallied together, pooling funds for a defense. Given the lengthy legal process that followed, one can only imagine that a significant amount was collected.

The first trial, in May 1879, was declared a mistrial after the jury found themselves unable to agree on a verdict. This in itself is somewhat incredible; trials of black men accused of killing white women typically resulted in a guilty verdict within a matter of minutes.

A second trial, less surprisingly, found John Bush guilty. The sentence: death. No doubt bolstered by the first trial's outcome, Bush's attorneys immediately filed an appeal. They also requested that the new trial be held in the local circuit court since the jury pool had only consisted of whites and, therefore, Bush had been denied a fair trial.

The guilty verdict was overturned and a new trial began. John's wife, Mary, was permitted to testify on his behalf when the case went to the circuit court, after the judge ruled that the couple was not legally married. The two had married before emancipation, when both were slaves. As such, their union was not considered legally binding. The two had not since undergone any formal ceremony, thus the marriage was declared void. With a new juror pool that still included no blacks, the circuit court trial resulted in another guilty verdict. The Kentucky Court of Appeals upheld the ruling.

The attorneys pressed on. In October 1882, the case of *John Bush v. Commonwealth of Kentucky* was heard in the United States Supreme Court. Three months later, the court issued its decision: "A denial to citizens of African descent, because of their race, of the right or privilege accorded to white citizens, of participating as jurors…is a discrimination…inconsistent with the [Fourteenth] amendment."

The Kentucky statute, which dictated that only white persons could serve on juries, was declared unconstitutional, in violation of the Fourteenth Amendment. The judgment of the appeals court was overruled. The murder case of John Bush was sent back to Fayette County.

The new Lexington trial took place in February 1884. Five years had elapsed since the shooting of Anna van Meter. An all-white jury was again selected from a pool of two hundred eligible citizens. Again, John Bush was found guilty. The Kentucky Court of Appeals upheld the verdict. Just at it looked as though the entire cycle of trials might repeat itself, the U.S. Supreme Court refused to hear the case a second time. This time, the justices felt reassured that there had been no discrimination in the selection of the jury; having no black people on the trial jury was not evidence that none had been selected for the original jury pool.

By November 21, 1884, John Bush had run out of appeals options. After five and a half years, no amount of legal or financial support could help. As he stood on the gallows, John maintained his innocence. He also alluded to the fact that Joseph van Meter had forced his wife to terminate a pregnancy, leaving one last tidbit to keep people guessing.

As a further point of interest, it would be more than fifty years before an African American would serve on a grand jury in Fayette County. In 1941, plumber George Johnson and tailor Charles Call Jr. would finally take that honor.

ISAAC TURNER

Kathleen Turner knew just who to turn to for help when Abe Ray beat her. She went to her son, Isaac. Outraged at the violence against his mother, the young Ike found Abe and shot him repeatedly. Despite a number of local citizens testifying to Turner's good character and Ray's drunken, violent nature, the young man was sentenced to death by hanging.

At 1:00 p.m., on July 28, 1882, Isaac Turner went to his death. Hopes of a reprieve from the governor were in vain, and he was led to the scaffold, where a crowd of fifty or so onlookers waited. Newspaper reports claim that "few thought him deserving of death." In fact, most sympathized with him for protecting his mother. But as one Iowa newspaper noted, "[T]he fact that Turner was a negro was sufficient in Kentucky" to ensure the death penalty rather than life in prison.

LYNCHINGS

Lynchings were commonplace in many parts of the state. Although the most oft-quoted number of lynchings in the state is 205 between 1882 and 1968, evidence indicates that the actual number may have been much higher, possibly even double the original figure. With the exceptions of Lexington and Louisville, towns in Kentucky were often no different to elsewhere in the South when it came to the brutality of "swift justice," as the practice was sometimes referred to. Lynchings did happen in the cities, too. George C. Wright's records show that more than one hundred men were lynched within a fifty-mile radius of Lexington.

Successive Kentucky governors worked to end lynching. At the end of the nineteenth century, William Bradley spoke out against the practice, and in 1897 lawmakers in the state passed a series of anti-lynching laws. Kentucky was one of the first states to pass such legislation. The law may have passed, but enacting it was another matter entirely, especially in areas where local law enforcement did not support the bill. Over the next forty years, at least seventy people around the state died from lynching.

THE KILLING OF WILLIAM MOORE

On a Sunday evening in November 1904, three black men entered Luigart's saloon in Lexington. Allegedly crying that they would "kill all white dogs," the men began to open fire on the white clientele. As one man, William Moore, attempted to hide behind a bourbon barrel, he was gunned down in cold blood. Garfield Smith, Ed Taylor and John Taylor were all arrested for the murder.

Word soon got out that the three men were being held at the jail, and a lynch mob was formed. Although fifty constables were already on duty to prevent any mob action, the threat was so severe that the county judge called in the militia. White gangs assembled in Brucetown (an African American community) and Bryant Station. In the downtown area, police placed barriers across the streets all around the jail and then created a human shield to prevent anyone gaining access. Another mob had formed in Bourbon County, headed by two brothers-in-law of the dead man; the widow had reportedly said that she wanted the men responsible to be lynched. Some three hundred men gathered at Gratz Park, but when confronted by the police, they were quick to disperse and go home.

It's hard to picture those days now, as one watches people mingle and children play. Yet little more than eighty years ago, downtown Lexington was the site of mass riots and military guards as one of Lexington's less favorable sides took center stage.

WILL LOCKETT

Geneva Hardman was just ten years old when her life was brutally snatched away. On February 4, 1920, as the little girl walked to school, just a few blocks from her home, she was attacked and beaten to death, her skull smashed by a rock. Her body was discovered in a nearby cornfield. The very same day, Will Lockett was arrested as a suspect. The African American World War I veteran confessed to killing Geneva while he was in custody. He was hurriedly sent to Frankfort to await trial; the threat of lynching was too great for him to remain in Lexington. Interestingly, this marks the first instance of officials in the South taking a stand against lynching.

A few days later, though, he was returned to Lexington to stand trial for the murder. The streets of downtown Lexington were packed with hundreds of people, some in town for court day and some in town with the hope of disrupting the trial and bringing their own form of justice to Will Lockett. Sensing that trouble might occur, Kentucky governor Edwin Murrow had the forethought to bring in a large number of National Guard troops to guard the

Cheapside Public Square, circa 1920. *Courtesy of Library of Congress.*

courthouse. The troops set up ropes along either side of the courthouse with the instruction to shoot anyone who crossed the line. Upon arriving with federal troops, Brigadier General Francis Marshall immediately declared martial law.

The trial took just thirty minutes. (The period of time from his arrest and indictment to trial was the quickest in Kentucky history.) As the guilty verdict was announced, chaos broke out. A cameraman outside the courthouse reportedly urged the waiting crowd to shout and wave their fists for the camera. Confused by the noise and thinking that an attack was in progress, several men rushed toward the doors of the courthouse, possibly in the hopes of seizing Lockett and hanging him on-site. Troops immediately opened fire, and some in the mob shot back.

The day's riots left 5 people dead and as many as 50 wounded. As night fell, 800 state and federal troops were patrolling the streets; another 400 were on their way to the city. Rumor of the impending arrival of a 1,500-strong lynching party from eastern Kentucky spread like wildfire, although this proved to be false. Media around the nation praised Governor Morrow for instilling order and avoiding a worse bloodbath.

Meanwhile, Lockett spent the night under heavy guard at the courthouse, while officials tried to let it be known that he had already left town. The next day, four hundred soldiers guarded Lockett on his trip to the state penitentiary at Eddyville, and more troops were stationed in the nearby town of Leitchfield, lest there be any further violence.

Stores in the downtown area were ordered to close their doors to prevent people congregating. (They would remain closed for several days.) The county superintendent insisted that schools would not reopen until "parents can feel it is safe to allow their children to go to and from school." Martial law in Lexington finally ended on February 23, after two weeks.

As for Will Lockett, there was more to him than was first suspected. A few days before his scheduled execution date, he reportedly confessed to the murders of three women. In 1912, he had strangled a white woman in Illinois; in 1917, the same fate befell a black woman in Evansville, Indiana; and in 1919, while he was in the army, he killed a third near Louisville. In addition, Lockett, whose real name was Petrie Kimbrough, had attempted his first assault on a white woman near his home in Todd County back in 1905.

If there had been any doubt about his fate for the murder of Geneva Hardman, news of these three additional murders brushed it aside. On March 11, Will Lockett, formerly Petrie Kimbrough, died in the electric chair.

ED HARRIS

Six years after the Will Lockett trial, Lexington would once more see a military presence around the courthouse to prevent a possible lynching. On February 2, 1926, Edward Harris faced trial for the murder of Clarence Bryant and his two children and for the rape of Mrs. Bryant. If Lockett's thirty-minute trial seemed expeditious, this one was doubly so. The judge decided to try Harris on the rape charge only, but that was enough to bring a sentence of death. The accused offered no defense, simply stating, "I brought it on myself." All told, the hearing and jury deliberation took only fifteen minutes.

But despite the speed with which the trial was conducted, it proved to be rather an expensive one. One thousand National Guard troops were brought into town two days earlier as a deterrent to any mob violence. Banks and other businesses were closed, and vehicles were prevented from entering the city. In the end, no mob assembled, but the trial cost $30,000. Harris pled guilty to all the charges against him and was hanged one month later in the Lexington jail courtyard.

Both the Lockett and Harris trials illustrate how the pretense of justice and avoidance of violent outbreaks superseded a fair trial. In both cases, officials had made it clear that the men would be found guilty. The trial was simply a formality. Execution was certain. When a black man was accused of a crime, concerns about proper legal procedure were abandoned. There are even stories of women telling police their attackers were black when they really were white. When Mildred Sorrell told police that she had been attacked by a black man in 1921, police questioned "suspicious" blacks. One suspects that all black men were considered suspicious. She later admitted that the perpetrator was actually a middle-aged white man. In the early decades of the twentieth century, the death penalty was imposed on African Americans in Fayette and surrounding counties for crimes as minimal as the theft of food and stealing six chickens. In many cases, even local black groups would not speak out about the lack of justice, perhaps for fear of repercussions.

White-on-black violence was a different matter—punishment was typically minimal, as in the 1900 murder of Robert Charles O'Hara Benjamin. A lawyer, journalist and poet, Benjamin was born in the British West Indies and educated at the University of Oxford. He traveled widely throughout South America and the Caribbean and lived for a while in New York before settling in Lexington. He was editor of the *Lexington Standard*, the city's African American newspaper. He was also an active organizer within the black community. He frequently denounced lynchings and helped with local voter registration drives. Michael Moynahan was a white Democrat. One day, Benjamin challenged him on the topic of his harassment of blacks, thereby preventing them from voting. An argument ensued, and Moynahan beat Benjamin about the head with his pistol. Benjamin insisted that the man be arrested, but he was released within an hour. That evening, as Benjamin returned home, he saw Moynahan waiting for him with a gun. The lawyer turned to flee but was shot in the back six times. The killer surrendered to police but pleaded not guilty. It was, he explained, a simple case of self-defense. The judge dismissed all charges against him. Benjamin's murder was the third case within one week of white men killing blacks. None ever went to trial. While Ed Harris awaited execution for the rape and murder of a white woman, Charles Merchant (a white man) was ruled insane and sent to an asylum after attacking two young black girls. Justice followed strict color boundaries.

THE '50S AND '60S: CIVIL RIGHTS

After the Supreme Court voted to desegregate schools in 1954, the struggle for equal rights soon spread to other parts of Lexington life. In 1954, the first class of African American students enrolled at the University of Kentucky. Transylvania would follow suit in 1963 when Lula Bee Morton became the first black student to enroll. By the end of the 1950s, Lexington residents had formed chapters of the National Association for the Advancement of Colored People (NAACP) and the Congress of Racial Equality (CORE). The local chapter of CORE was led by Professor William Reichert, of the University of Kentucky. When he returned to Lexington from Minnesota in 1956, he described the local racial situation as "absolutely unacceptable." The city buses were already desegregated, but lunch counters, restrooms and waiting rooms were closed to blacks or heavily segregated. In 1960, members participated in a series of sit-ins at lunch counters along Main Street.

Unlike in other parts of the South, protestors faced little violence; the most common act they faced was having water tipped over them. Leaders of the groups later recalled that the city judge and police were supportive of their actions. However, local newspapers refused to publish letters from CORE that would explain members' actions and motives. Newspaper editorials indicated opposition to what they saw as communist disruption of downtown Lexington. One notable protest occurred in 1961. The Boston Celtics were scheduled to play an exhibition game at town but found their black players barred from service at a local coffee shop. They promptly left town on the next plane, leaving a handful of white players to play. Within a few years, restaurants and theaters around town had ended their policies of discrimination. Reichert left Lexington around this time, with many suspecting that the university disapproved of his civil rights activities.

Lexington was not entirely without violence during this era. After news of Martin Luther King's assassination reached town, some neighborhoods saw outbreaks of arson and vandalism. A few months later, the only black pharmacy in town was bombed; the Ku Klux Klan claimed credit.

Chapter 6
TROUBLES AT TRANSY

At the far end of Gratz Park, a few blocks from downtown Lexington, stands the imposing Old Morrison. Six enormous columns line the front of the Greek Revival–style building, which is the heart of Transylvania University. Originally, the building contained a chapel, a library and classrooms; today it is used primarily for administrative offices. In its history, the halls of Morrison have been used not just for learning and worship. It was an army hospital during the Civil War, both Union and Confederate.

Not long after the pioneers established Lexington, Transylvania (or Transy, as it is affectionately known) planted roots in the town. It was founded in 1780, the first college west of the Alleghenies and the sixteenth in the nation at the time. The Commonwealth of Virginia provided eight thousand acres of lands confiscated from the British as a site for a public school. The official charter was granted three years later.

Transylvania University played a key role in Lexington's early development. The university was as prestigious as both Harvard and Yale, and one cannot deny that its presence drew some of the finest minds to the town. It originally was home to a law school, a seminary, a medical school and a college of arts and sciences. Among early supporters of the institution were George Washington, Thomas Jefferson, John Adams and the infamous Aaron Burr. Henry Clay taught law here, and Constantine Rafinesque taught biology and languages. The list of famous alumni is even more impressive: two U.S. vice presidents, two Supreme Court

Old Morrison at Transylvania University. *Courtesy of Library of Congress.*

justices, fifty U.S. senators, more than one hundred U.S. representatives and multiple governors and ambassadors. No wonder Lexington was called the Athens of the West, when some of the foremost movers and shakers of the day gathered here.

Transy has also seen its share of characters. Drs. Drake, Dudley and Richardson were all medical pioneers in their respective fields, but the decision to fight a duel (as described in an earlier chapter) turned heads all around town. In this chapter, I will look at one of Transy's most colorful characters, a brilliant mind who is said to have placed a curse on the school and its president. I will also recall one of Transy's most tragic moments.

CONSTANTINE RAFINESQUE

Transylvania University's campus has seen some colorful characters come and go over the years. One of the most memorable was a botanist and writer by the name of Constantine Samuel Rafinesque. He was born in 1783 in Constantinople to a French tradesman and a German/Greek/Turkish (sources vary) mother. Most of his childhood was spent in the French seaport of Marseilles, where he taught himself everything from Latin to botany.

In 1802, he visited the United States for the first time, traveling through Pennsylvania and Delaware with his brother. After gathering quite a collection of plant specimens for his research, Rafinesque returned to Europe, settling on the Italian isle of Sicily. Clearly having learned much from his father, the young man was so successful in business that by the age of twenty-five he was able to retire and devote himself fully to his studies. Although barely appreciated for his work while alive, modern scholars remain convinced that he was far ahead of his time in biology, geology, meteorology and a host of other areas.

At some point, Rafinesque had taken a common-law wife, and the couple had a son. However, after the son died in 1815, Rafinesque left his wife and moved to the United States again. Sadly, his extensive collection of books and plant and shell specimens were all lost when the ship he traveled on hit trouble near the Connecticut coast. Undeterred, he began to rebuild his collection while living in New York.

In 1819, Rafinesque was offered a botany professorship at Transy, and so he packed his bags and moved south. In addition to teaching, he continued to catalogue plant and wildlife specimens, but his published work was often ignored by other academics. It seems his written word was as erratic and colorful as both his personal and professional lives.

Professor Rafinesque was no doubt a colorful character around Lexington. Although the fledgling city had other French settlers—including the confectioner Monsieur Giron and the Mentelles, who opened a French school at Transy, as well as a private girls' school where the young Mary Todd was educated—one suspects that none of the residents was quite as gossip-worthy as the flamboyant Rafinesque. In addition to teaching botany, he taught French and Italian and served as the university librarian, all the while continuing to collect and categorize new plant specimens and write about his discoveries.

Constantine Rafinesque was as eccentric as he was learned. His spirit is rumored to still walk the halls of Old Morrison.

Many things came naturally to him, but teaching may not have been one of them. Perhaps he felt that classes interrupted his time for making new scholarship. Perhaps he was simply unable to relate to those around him. One thing is sure: students complained that he rarely appeared in class; when he did, he spoke at such a rate and in such an advanced manner that few could understand what he was talking about.

There was one other rumored problem. That other famously multitalented Renaissance man, Benjamin Franklin, was well known to have had an appetite for the ladies that was almost as voracious as his appetite for learning. Did Constantine Rafinesque share similar appetites?

Transylvania University was headed by a long line of Presbyterians until the Yale-educated Unitarian minister Horace Holley was brought in to serve as president in 1818. Under his tenure, the university soon became one of the best in the nation, contributing to Lexington's reputation as the Athens of the West. Enrollment quadrupled, and the medical school flourished. Holley's wife, Mary, thrived in the academic environment, enjoying lively intellectual discussions with the faculty. Given that Mary Holley was a good Christian woman, it might be a little hard to believe that she may have fallen for the charms of Rafinesque. Or perhaps not. Perhaps it is quite easy to see where a deep friendship could have developed as she sat enthralled by his passion for scholarship. He was reportedly a frequent guest at the home of the University president, but one suspects that the man of the house was not the issuer of some invitations. Holley wrote to his brother: "Rafinesque writes so much nonsense." He even warned the publisher that he should probably cease allowing Rafinesque to publish if he wanted to keep his business prosperous.

Even so, Mary Holley certainly spent much time with the European botanist, and rumors began to circulate that the two were sharing a romantic liaison. Was Mary swept off her feet by the passionate Frenchman? Or did she simply enjoy spending time with the intellectuals who abounded on the Transy campus? We shall most likely never know if there was any justification to the rumors.

By 1826, Rafinesque had worn out his welcome in Lexington. Holley grew tired of his rambling scholarship, lack of devotion to teaching and befriending of his wife. In a heated argument, he fired the professor, who uttered a curse upon the entire university and Holley and then stormed out. Yet the story of Rafinesque and Transylvania University does not end there.

Within the next few years, Horace Holley resigned from the university and died of yellow fever while on a vacation cruise from New Orleans (their new home) to New York. Meanwhile, Morrison College burned to the ground. This combination of events gave rise to the legend of the Rafinesque curse.

But what of the eclectic scholar of botany, linguistics and other subjects too numerous to mention? Following his dismissal from Transy, he moved back to Philadelphia, where he continued to write and where he became the first person to decipher the ancient Mayan language. He died in 1840 from stomach cancer. Although not financially ruined, as many have claimed, he had spent large parts of his fortune on publishing. Much of his work and his massive collections of specimens were destroyed after his death. Only decades later did scholars recognize his work for the genius contained therein. In 1924, what were thought to be his remains were moved to a crypt in the basement of the rebuilt Morrison College. They are probably the remains of Mary Passimore, who was buried on top of Rafinesque later in the nineteenth century, as was the habit in crowded burial grounds. The tomb is there to this day, bearing the inscription, "Honor to whom honor is overdue."

Today, some still believe that the ghost of Constantine Samuel Rafinesque haunts the campus of Transylvania University, making an appearance every seven years. Students at the institution celebrate Rafinesque Week each year before Halloween. A raffle apparently allows the winner to spend Halloween night in the crypt. In addition, the school's dining hall is named the Rafskellar in his honor. In one form or another, the spirit of Rafinesque lives on.

THE KILLING OF BETTY GAIL BROWN

A far more tragic event in Transy's history took place one October night in 1961.

Betty Gail Brown was a nineteen-year-old from Lexington, part of the university's five-hundred-strong student body. A sophomore, she had won a scholarship to attend Transylvania but still lived at home with her parents. Betty was a popular student, a member of the college pep squad who taught Sunday school at her local church. On October 26, 1961, she stayed late on campus, studying for a biology midterm with some friends at one of the women's dorms. It was a pleasantly warm fall evening. Betty chatted and studied with friends until shortly after midnight, when she bid them goodnight and returned to her car. As she drove out of campus, she saw another classmate and pulled over to chat for a few minutes before telling him that she was headed home.

By 2:51 a.m., Betty's dad was getting worried. She still was not home, and even with exams looming, this was not like Betty. He called the police. Lexington police didn't have to look very hard to find her car—there it was in the main campus parking lot. Inside they found the body of Betty Gail Brown. Someone had used her bra to strangle her. The back doors of the car were locked, but bloodstains and a dent in the dashboard indicated a struggle. Transylvania University had a murder on its hands.

While the campus went into a flurry of panic, police speculated about the attack. Was the killer someone she knew? Someone she had offered a ride home? Or had they hidden in the back seat of her car, waiting to make their move as she drove home? There was no evidence of a sexual assault, but how had the killer removed her bra? Betty's blouse was still neatly tucked into her shorts. Her purse was on the seat beside her, ruling out robbery as a motive. Clues were few, and there were no witnesses at that late hour. A few residents at the local men's dorm said that they had heard a scream somewhere outside at about 1:15 a.m., and other locals reported seeing a strange man attempting to hitchhike his way out of town not much later. Despite interviews with several ex-boyfriends, every lead turned cold.

It stayed cold for quite some time. One year later, police in New York arrested a former Transy student, found dressed as a woman with a gun and newspaper clippings of the murder in his possession. Although they could charge him with impersonating a woman, and with violation of firearms law, there was nothing to link him to the death of Betty Gail Brown.

Four years after the crime, police finally thought that they had got their man. A horse groom by the name of Alex Arnold admitted to strangling Betty. In a statement given to Oregon and, later, Kentucky police, he claimed that he had seen Betty and another woman in the parked car and had asked them for a light for his cigarette. Not only did they refuse, they began to cuss at him as well. Increasingly angry by their insults, Arnold said that he had climbed into the back of the car. The other woman fled while he strangled Betty with the bra, which had been laying over the back of the seat. He was returned to Lexington to face trial.

Arnold's defense argued that the admission of guilt had been provided when the accused was under the influence of alcohol, but prosecutors noted that he had repeated the same statement when sober. Even so, the trial deadlocked, with the jury unable to reach a consensus after the defending attorney noted several inconsistencies between his statement and the actual crime. Arnold got the location of the car wrong, and his insistence that the bra was on the car seat conflicted with evidence that it had been ripped from Betty's body. Other errors included the number of buttons fastened on her blouse and how he had managed to lock the car doors. One remaining mystery was the identity of the second person in the vehicle. Arnold claimed that Betty and the other woman, a blonde with glasses, had been kissing, yet no other woman ever came forward. (Of course, that might be explained away by attitudes toward same-sex relationships, especially in the South, in the 1960s.) A second trial never happened. Charges were dropped after doubts about Arnold's credibility (and sanity) grew with the revelation that spots on the wall apparently talked to him.

And so the murder of Betty Gail Brown slowly faded in the city's memory. Rumors persisted that Betty's mother, Quincy, and other family members suspected someone and carefully followed him but did not have enough evidence to prove their theories.

By the dawn of the twenty first century, DNA testing and forensics had made enormous progress, offering new hope to the detectives who had never quite been able to let Betty's murder rest. In 2010, they found similarities between the murder of Betty Gail Brown and a 1968 murder in Michigan. The accused in the Michigan murder was Nolan Ray George, a native of London, Kentucky. George held prior convictions for the strangulation of two young women and had confessed to a third. At the same time, police started looking into another possible suspect, a recently arrested serial killer in California. His preferred method of killing was strangulation. George, though, was of particular interest, and police were hoping that evidence collected from the original crime scene might contain traces of DNA that were usable. At the time of writing, Nolan Ray George has not officially been charged with the murder of Betty Gail Brown. However, police remain hopeful that DNA may be able to lead to a positive identification of the killer. Sadly, Miss Brown's parents passed away before the case could be solved.

Chapter 7

WICKED SPORTS

There is a local saying that in Kentucky everyone follows the three Bs: the Bible, bourbon and basketball. The order of those three may change according to the particular circumstances, but in Lexington, basketball may well be second only to religion. Visitors cannot help but notice on game days the swathe of blue everywhere they go.

Twice a year, in April and October, the city becomes engulfed by another sporting interest. When the Keeneland meets are in session, traffic grinds to a halt and restaurants overflow. This is Kentucky, after all. The horse is king.

So it will no doubt surprise many to know that, while Lexington may be known among sports fans for its college basketball and horse racing, it was a golfer who is at the center of the city's most wicked sporting crime.

MARION MILEY

Marion Miley was born in Philadelphia in 1914. Her father, Fred, was a golf pro who had never managed to break into the major tournaments. His talents for the game also encompassed teaching, club making and course design, and so the family moved from around the country, from one club to another, with Fred teaching the sport and bringing in some extra money from his gambling successes. Considering his love for the sport, one might imagine that Miley had been groomed from an early age, as tots today so often are. On the contrary, she did not pick up her first golf club until the age of twelve.

In 1929, Fred accepted a position as head golf pro at the Lexington Country Club, and the family moved to Kentucky. Marion's mother, Elsie, took on the role of club manager. Meanwhile, Fred helped Marion develop her fledgling skills on the green. She was a fast learner and had a good teacher.

After completing high school, Marion enrolled in Florida State Women's College, where she planned to study physical education and music, the perfect combination, it seemed, for a future teacher. Fate—and golf—would intervene. After winning the 1931 and 1932 Kentucky Women's Amateur tournaments, Marion decided that it was time to drop out of college and aim for the professional golfing ranks.

In 1933, she qualified for the U.S. Women's Amateur. Disappointingly, she lost in the first round, but Marion Miley was not going to be deterred. She was on her way to the top.

America's Great Depression was fully underway. These were bleak times for the country. The future was also rather bleak for female golfers, given that there was no professional circuit. The amateur circuit proved to be incredibly popular, however, and people flocked to watch the tournaments, if only to forget their own troubles for a while.

Marion set off on the women's golf circuit, traveling from one tournament to the next. The players were well treated, and when not playing golf, they enjoyed parties, dinners and interviews with the press. Having grown up in country clubs, Marion took the fame in stride. In 1934, she won both the Riviera Championship and the Augusta Invitational, going on to earn a place on the 1934 USA Curtis Cup team. (As the team's alternate, she did not get to play.)

Over the next few years, she continued to win tournaments. Hollywood stars Bing Crosby and W.C. Fields watched her win the Mexican Women's Open. Bing, an avid golfer, was reportedly very impressed with her skills and promised that they would play together one day. After breezing through several tournaments in Florida, Marion won the Western Championship in both 1935 and 1936. Still, she could not make it to the top of the nation's golfing elite. When she was named to the Curtis Cup team, she was again relegated to the position of alternate, much to the chagrin of the British press, who wanted to see this tall, elegant young American woman play.

It was not until 1938 that Marion Miley was finally given the opportunity to play in the Curtis Cup. She beat her British rival, Elsie Corlett, and the U.S. women won the championship. Sadly, because of the Second World War, it would be the last Curtis Cup until 1948. Although no one knew it at the time, Marion would never get to play for the team again.

Marion was determined to become the best female golfer in the nation. In a 1940 interview with a member of the Louisville press, when asked about her future, the young star replied, "To become the best woman golfer in the world. Then to challenge the men." Her goal of eventually outdoing the men was an oft-repeated one. While in England, a London reported had once asked her how it felt to be among the top female golfers in the world. "Why stop with women?" came her reply. Described on the green as "cool under fire—a golfer without nerves," Marion Miley was a darling of the press.

Miley continued to make her way up the golfing ranks, although the title of U.S. Women's Amateur still eluded her. A bout of tendonitis interfered with her game in 1941, and so in September she returned home to the Lexington Country Club for a few days of rest after a tournament loss. Her mother, Elsie, was busily preparing for a dance at the club that Saturday. Marion helped with the preparations but chose to spend the evening out of the limelight. Instead, she visited a friend before returning to her apartment. She and her mother were the only residents at the country club. Her father, Fred, was now living and working at a club in Cincinnati.

The Ben-Mar Sanitarium stood a quarter or a mile or so from the Lexington Country Club, across Paris Pike. Manager J.M. Giles was cozy in his bed when he was woken at 4:15 a.m. on Sunday, September 28. At first he thought that there might be an emergency with one of the residents, but he soon realized that the noise the awoke him was the doorbell. Hurrying to open the front door, he found Elsie Miley, covered in blood. She collapsed in his arms. A trail of blood showed that she had crawled all the way from her apartment, desperately seeking help.

By the time the police arrived, she was unconscious. As an ambulance took her to St. Joseph's Hospital (then at its old location on West Second Street), police went across the street to the country club. What they found was a scene of devastation and murder. The body of Marion Miley lay on the floor, bullet wounds to the head and back. She died before she reached the hospital.

Elsie regained consciousness briefly at the hospital, and police were able to piece together what had happened. At about 2:25 a.m., intruders had cut the electrical and telephone wires. They then kicked in the door of Mrs. Miley's apartment. Holding her at gunpoint, they demanded the takings from a dance held at the club the previous evening. Elsie told police that they wanted "only money." When the money was not as much as they had expected, they became angry. Suddenly, one of the men bludgeoned Elsie about the head with an iron weight from the kitchen. She screamed, and several shots were fired, hitting her in the abdomen. At this point, Marion, woken by the noise, rushed to her mother's apartment. The gunman shot the golf star twice, first in the head and then in the back as she fell. Elsie was able to give only the vaguest description of the attackers before lapsing back into unconsciousness. She died of her wounds on October 1. Police were now faced with a double murder investigation. The site yielded only a few clues: a button from a man's coat, a few strands of blond hair and a .38 slug. Any fingerprints were too smeared in blood to be truly useful.

The murders made national news, and a massive manhunt got underway. The Lexington Country Club immediately put up a reward of $1,000. Club members added $700. Kentucky governor Keen Johnson also contributed to the fund. It is said that Hollywood star Bing Crosby, who never got to play his round of golf with Marion, donated $5,000 to find the men responsible.

One of the earliest witnesses to come forward was seventeen-year-old Hugh Cramer, a newspaper delivery boy. He told police that sometime between 3:00 and 3.30 a.m. he had seen a car parked by the side entrance of the club. He knew Mrs. Miley and her daughter and knew both of their vehicles. This car was not theirs. Police put out a bulletin for a Buick with Jefferson County (Louisville) plates.

Louisville police were soon able to trace the car to a local dealer. He told them that he had recently sold the car to local nightclub owner, Robert Anderson. Anderson owned the Cat and the Fiddle. A stocky man, with a "round, cherubic face," he was well liked by his clientele, mostly soldiers from the nearby army bases. Whiskey was half price for men in uniform, and they also knew that if they were short in cash, Bob would give them a hot meal. But what would he want with the Mileys? As it happens, he had reported the Buick stolen.

The car would be found in Fort Worth, Texas, on October 9. The occupant was Thomas C. Penney, a Lexington man with a criminal past. He had been convicted of auto theft and armed robbery and was currently on parole. One of his jobs was that of drink deliveryman to the Lexington Country Club. To thicken the plot further, he was an acquaintance of Anderson's—the two were once inmates at the Kentucky State Reformatory in LaGrange, Kentucky. After confessing to his involvement in the crime, which he claimed was a robbery gone wrong, Penney was extradited back to Kentucky for further questioning about the murders of Marion and Elsie Miley. He named his accomplice as Robert Anderson.

Meanwhile, Lexington police looked at the involvement of a third man. Since day one, they had suspected that the robbery might be an inside job—how else could they know about the dances and the cash or be able to enter the building undetected? Raymond "Skeeter" Baxter was brought in for questioning. The twenty-eight-year-old worked as a greenskeeper at the club and often slept in the caddy house. One journalist described the erstwhile drug addict thus: "[H]is pock-marked face, deeply sunken cheeks, prominent off-center nose, and melancholy brown eyes gave him the look of an emaciated weasel."

Once Penney was extradited back to Kentucky, the story of the crime was pieced together. Baxter claimed that he had gone to a local tavern the night of the dance, and then, rather than going back to his spot at the country club, he had gone to the home of his girlfriend, former prostitute turned actress Penny Smith. At about 2:00 a.m., he returned to the club, where he met the two robbers, helping them get into the building and showing them where the electricity and telephone wires were located. He remained adamant that this was to be a robbery only; he had told them about the Saturday dances. After the dances, Mrs. Miley could have as much as $15,000 in her apartment until she took it to the bank on Monday.

Penney arrived in Lexington, and after confessing, he turned state's evidence, pointing the finger at Robert Anderson as his accomplice. He claimed that the two men had expected to find more than $5,000 but came away with less than $145. They buried the murder weapons in a Louisville amusement park. Then, at Anderson's suggestion, Penney took the Buick and drove first to Florida and then to Texas.

Interestingly, Baxter corroborated Penney's story, except for one fact. When asked about Penney's accomplice, he replied, "Who did Penney say it was?" He would follow this pattern of behavior several times in the upcoming months, never pointing the finger himself but rather waiting to see how Penney had named and then simply agreeing.

Anderson denied any part in the crime. He argued that Penney was trying to falsely accuse him as payback for an earlier disagreement. Penney was in the business of hijacking trucks of liquor as they left local distilleries. Sometimes Anderson would buy the whiskey, but he claimed that the most recent batch was bad. He had refused to buy it, and Penney, angry at being turned away, was willing to implicate him in murder to get his revenge. Anderson even produced witnesses to corroborate his story that he was at the Cat and the Fiddle earlier that Saturday evening. Of the three men, Anderson was the only one who continually proclaimed his innocence. It was this ongoing denial of involvement that would keep the jury deliberating.

As Christmas 1941 drew near, Robert Anderson, Thomas Penney and Raymond Baxter stood trial for the murders of the two Miley women. It took a jury only minutes to find Penney and Baxter guilty. In Anderson's case, it took close to twenty-four hours, but when the verdict came, it was one of guilt, too. All three men were sentenced to die in the electric chair.

One might expect that to be the end of the story, but the question of Anderson's guilt dragged on. In February 1942, the men were sent to Eddyville Prison, where they would remain until executed. It seems that during this time, Penney underwent a conversion and became a member of the Catholic faith. Shortly thereafter, he confessed to the prison warden that he had lied about Anderson as a means of getting revenge against him for their earlier argument. His real accomplice was a man by the name of Buford Stewart. The warden interviewed Baxter, trying to substantiate the claims. As before, Baxter asked who Penney had said the accomplice was and then agreed that it was Stewart. There was just one problem: Buford Stewart was killed in a brawl in February 1942, leaving police unable to question him.

Nevertheless, Penney had confessed, and so Anderson quickly petitioned for a stay of execution until a new trial could be held. This put state attorneys in something of a quandary. They could not execute Baxter and Penney while Anderson was awaiting an appeal; they were the key witnesses. There was little to do but grant a stay of execution for all three.

Two weeks later, Thomas Penney called a news conference at which he announced that he would never say one more word about the Miley case. That included testifying at Anderson's new hearing. Since the court refused to consider Penney's written deposition, the appeal was denied.

The executions took place at Eddyville Penitentiary on February 26, 1943. A last-minute plea for clemency on the part of Baxter, on the grounds that he was a simple-minded man, was denied. Robert Anderson was first to his death. As he left his cell, he yelled, "Tom Penney, you miserable son of a bitch…I'll be waiting for you in hell." He maintained his innocence to the last. Skeeter Baxter was last to the chair. When asked if he had any last words, he whispered, "I'm going home."

It was the final words of the second man to die, Thomas Penney, that kept many guessing. The Catholic convert had changed his story several times. Would he now reveal the truth? Was Anderson really the man who had pulled the trigger? Or was he an unfortunate victim of the justice system? As Penney was strapped into the chair, he looked at Eddyville warden Jesse Buchanan: "Warden, I have told you the truth. Publish it." With that, the lever was pulled, the lights flickered and all was done.

In a letter to Warden Buchanan, read after Penney's death, the man revealed that Anderson was indeed his accomplice. The nightclub owner had offered to take care of Penney's ailing mother financially if he said that Anderson was innocent. The simple-minded Skeeter Baxter had provided a room layout and helped them access the building—nothing more.

The promising career of a sports star may have ended prematurely, but Marion's memory lives on at the Lexington Country Club, which hosts the Marion Miley Invitational each year.

ADOLPH RUPP AND THE WILDCATS

It's hard to live in Lexington and not like basketball, or rather college basketball. When the University of Kentucky Wildcats play, the city becomes a sea of blue, and every TV in town seems to be tuned in to watch the game. No wonder this part of the country is nicknamed the Big Blue Nation.

The hiring of a new basketball coach grips Wildcat fans, who are some of the most enthusiastic fans in college sports. Over the years, the university has seen some outstanding coaches and some dire failures, but one man stands out above them all. He remains the bar by which all other coaches are measured. He is the Man in the Brown Suit.

Adolph Rupp was born in 1901 in Halstead, Kansas, one of six children in a family of German Mennonites. His father died when Adolph was just nine years old, so the oldest son took over managing the family farm. The children all worked on the farm when they were not at school. Rupp developed an interest in basketball when he was very young; Halstead won two consecutive Kansas state high school titles. The Rupp boys played with a homemade basketball. Years later, Adolph Rupp would play on the Halstead High School basketball team, but when he went to college, he remained a reserve for the University of Kansas Jayhawks. As a reserve, he spent a lot of time on the sidelines, observing and learning from the team coaches. Kansas was one of the top teams in the country, so he was learning from the best.

After a one-year stint teaching in Kansas, Rupp taught wrestling at a high school in Iowa. Although he knew nothing about the sport, he read a book on the subject and led the team to a state title. From there, he moved to Freeport, Illinois, where he taught history and economics and coached high school basketball. In a move that would be significant later in his career, Coach Rupp allowed William Moseley to play. He was the first African American student to play at the school. Some claim that Rupp was forced to leave for daring to play a black player in the 1920s; others say it was because he did not win a championship. Either way, the issue of race would haunt him throughout his career.

In 1930, Adolph Rupp went from teaching high school basketball in Illinois to being the head coach at the University of Kentucky. The next forty-two years of his career would be with the Wildcats. Team training was hard and focused. The coach and his assistants wore starched uniforms, and his cardinal rule was, "Don't speak unless you can improve the silence." If a player messed up, they could expect a harsh rebuke in his Kansas twang. He once told a player, "You're nothing but a Shetland pony in a studhorse derby." Rupp's tactics paid off. During the Rupp era of Kentucky basketball, the Wildcats won four NCAA championships, one NIT title, five Sugar Bowl championships, twenty-seven SEC season titles and thirteen SEC tournaments. They appeared in twenty NCAA tournaments, with six trips to the Final Four. In addition to becoming beloved by fans for his record, Rupp was also popular because

Adolph Rupp and the "Fabulous Five." *Courtesy of University of Kentucky.*

of his choice to use local talent. More than 80 percent of his recruits were Kentuckians. At every game, Rupp could be seen on the sidelines, wearing a brown suit (he had worn blue once while coaching at Freeport, but the team lost and he always wore brown for games from then on).

There were several controversies to hit Kentucky in the '50s and '60s. First was the issue of point-shaving. In 1952, a New York grand jury charged thirty-three college players from around the country with accepting money in return for shaving points. Among those who confessed were three Kentucky players, members of the 1948 and 1949 NCAA Championship teams. Rupp had always bragged that gamblers could not touch his boys, and when news of their actions broke, it is said that Rupp would not talk to the players involved for another twenty years, so great was his sense of betrayal. Also in 1952, the Wildcats were forced to sit out an entire season as punishment for rules violations. UK's reputation was tarnished, and there was some speculation that Rupp might be replaced, but the rumors proved to be unfounded. The Cats came back with a vengeance the following season, not losing a single game. But they did not go to the NCAA tournament that year; Rupp declined when three of his star players were declared ineligible. He felt that their winning season said more about their skill than any one tournament could.

One controversy that continues to rile up basketball fans on both sides is whether Rupp was a racist. He was coaching during the '60s, and the question of racial integration continues to haunt the Kentucky team. This reached a head in 1966 with the now famous Kentucky–Texas Western NCAA title game. The all-white Kentucky team faced an all-black Texas team in what has often been referred to as "the *Brown v. Board of Education* of college basketball." Looking back, the UK players have said that race was not an issue at the time of the matchup. In a 2005 WKYT documentary, Tommy Kron recalled:

> *I'm very proud of what we did that year. I'm very proud that we got there. I'm disappointed that we didn't bring the title home. The controversy is a separate issue. It wasn't there at that time. So I mean it wasn't a part of the game for me.*

Indeed, when reporting the outcome of the game, which Texas Western won 72–65, not once is the race of any team member on either side mentioned. Race did not seem to be mentioned until 1991, when *Sports Illustrated* put out an issue to commemorate the twenty-fifth anniversary of the game. Referring to the former governor of Alabama, the magazine's

Seth Davis called Rupp "the George Wallace" of basketball. One journalist covering the Kentucky–Texas Western game, Frank Deford, said that he had heard Rupp using a number of racial insults in the locker room during halftime. Players have insisted that this was not the case, and some have questioned whether Deford was even in the locker room. Later, Deford said that so much of that particular game had been taken out of context that he would no longer discuss it. Was this a case of revisionist history, or was it a case of a long-hidden truth coming to light?

Let us not forget that Rupp had apparently risked his career when, as a coach at Freeport, he recruited and played an African American. In 1951, Kentucky were scheduled to play St. John's. Rupp reportedly wrote to the sports editor of the *Herald-Leader*, asking that Kentucky fans treat the team's black player with the same kindness and respect that they show all other visitors. Newspaper reports as far back as 1961 quote Rupp expressing a desire to integrate his team, saying that he planned to recruit black players, a move that would lead to the end of segregation in SEC athletics. (The coach later said that he had been misunderstood and that he made no apparent moves to recruit nonwhite players.)

On the other hand, the *New York Times* used to tell the story that he wanted sports editors to put asterisks by the names of black players so he knew which ones not to pick. A coach at another university reported having a conversation in which Rupp said that the problem with college basketball was "too many black players." The same coach would later claim not to recall the incident. Tim Bassett, one of the first African American players in the SEC, claims that Rupp approached him after a game, telling him that he didn't belong in the SEC and that they would get him when he came to Kentucky. One month later, when the Bulldogs arrived in Lexington, Bassett says an effigy of him was hanging in the visitors' dressing room.

It was reported that Rupp wanted to recruit Perry Wallace but that Wallace was put off by the fact that Rupp seemed "conspicuously absent" during the recruitment process. Knowing how risky it could be for a black player to travel through the Deep South, Wallace wondered "how I could place my life on the line when there is someone who is not willing to make personal contact with me." Instead, he chose to play for Vanderbilt as the first African American player in the SEC. The University of Kentucky finally welcomed its first African American in 1970, with the arrival of Tom Payne.

Was Rupp racist? There is probably a little revisionism on both sides. There are those who will say that he tried his best to include black players but was working within a system that did not welcome integration, and there are those who will say that he wanted to keep his team white for as long as possible. The truth is probably somewhere in between. Certainly, he was not the only coach to play an all-white team in the late 1960s.

By 1972, Rupp had reached the mandatory UK retirement age, and he bid farewell to the team. He remained in Lexington until his death in December 1977. Just minutes earlier, Kentucky had defeated Kansas at the arena bearing the coach's name. One thing is certain, without Adolph Rupp, it is unlikely that UK basketball would be the success that it is today. When he first arrived in Lexington, the Wildcats were a decent team; by the time he retired, they dominated the world of college basketball.

The issue of race and Kentucky basketball reared its head again in 1997 when Tubby Smith became the university's first black basketball coach. When asked about Adolph Rupp, he replied:

> *I know there have been a lot of people who thought he was a racist. But I think the times can dictate how people act—where you're brought up, how you're brought up. If he was a racist, he wasn't alone in this country. I'm never going to judge anybody…That's a long time ago, too…You learn from the past, and you go on.*

And so, too, with a past that is checkered with the good and the bad, Lexington goes on.

BIBLIOGRAPHY

Alvey, R. Gerald. *Kentucky Bluegrass Country*. Jackson: University Press of Mississippi, 1992.

American Slavery As It Is: Testimony of a Thousand Witnesses. New York: American Anti-Slavery Society, 1839.

Baker, Jean H. *Mary Todd Lincoln: A Biography*. New York: W.W. Norton, 1987.

Baltimore Herald. "Arguing for Madeline." April 14, 1894.

Baltimore Sun. "Killed in a Political Quarrel." November 17, 1887.

Benton, Thomas Hart. *Thirty Years View: A History of the Working of the American Government for Thirty Years*. New York: D. Appleton and Co., 1854.

Berry, Stephen. *House of Abraham*. New York: Houghton Mifflin, 2007.

Billings, Dwight B., Gurney Norman and Katherine Ledford, eds. *Confronting Appalachian Stereotypes*. Lexington: University Press of Kentucky, 1999.

Bolin, James Duane. *Bossism and Reform in a Southern City: Lexington, Kentucky, 1880–1940*. Lexington: University Press of Kentucky, 2000.

Buchanan, William J. *Execution Eve*. Far Hills, NJ: New Horizon Press, 1993.

Chamberlain, Ryan. *Pistols, Politics, and the Press: Dueling in 19ᵗʰ Century American Journalism*. Jefferson, NC: McFarland, 2008.

Chicago Daily Tribune. "Breckinridge's Line of Defense." September 14, 1893.

———. "Clarkson on the Lexington Tragedy." November 19, 1889.

———. "Club Employee Admits Role in Miley Slayings." October 19, 1941.

———. "Compares Vice of Big Cities." November 29, 1900.

———. "He Never Made Love." March 31, 1894.

———. "The Lesson of the Kentucky Tragedy." November 15, 1889.

———. "Lexington Quiet as Negro Goes to Death Cell." February, 11, 1920.

———. "Masons to Expel Breckinridge." July 14, 1894.

———. "Mrs. Blackburn Aids Miss Pollard." February 20, 1894.

———. "Two Bandits Slay Woman Golf Star." September 29, 1941.

———. "Watterson on Kentucky Barbarism." November 22, 1889.

Clarke, Lewis Garrard, and Milton Clarke. *Narratives of the Sufferings of Lewis and Milton Clarke, Sons of a Soldier of the Revolution, During a Captivity of More Than Twenty Years Among the Slaveholders of Kentucky, One of the So-Called Christian States of North America*. Boston, MA: Bela Marsh, 1846. Part of the Documenting the American South Collection at the University of North Carolina at Chapel Hill.

Coleman, J. Winston, Jr. *Double Murder at the Lexington Country Club*. Lexington, KY: Winburn Press, 1981.

———. *Famous Kentucky Duels*. Lexington, KY: Henry Clay Press, 1969.

———. *Stage-Coach Days in the Bluegrass*. Lexington: University Press of Kentucky, 1995.

———. *The Trotter-Wickliffe Duel*. Frankfort, KY: Roberts Printing Co., 1950.

Craig, Berry. *True Tales of Old-Time Kentucky Politics*. Charleston, SC: The History Press, 2009.

Denton, Sally. *The Bluegrass Conspiracy*. New York: Doubleday, 1990.

Detroit Free Press. "Miss Pollard's Future." April 16, 1894.

Ethington Family Organization. *The Trouble at the Courthouse*. Record compiled October 2008. Unpublished family history but available from http://ethington.org/REPORTS.aspx.

Fairbank, Calvin, and Laura Smith Haviland. *Rev. Calvin Fairbank During Slavery Times*. Chicago: R.R. McCabe and Co., 1890.

Harrison, Lowell Hayes, and James C. Klotter. *A New History of Kentucky*. Lexington: University Press of Kentucky, 1997.

Heidler, David S., and Jeanne T. Heidler. *Henry Clay: The Essential American*. New York: Random House, 2010.

Henry, M.J. "Kentucky's Early Lithotomists." http://www.innominatesociety. com/Articles/Kentuckys%20Early%20Lithotomists.htm.

Hines, Emilee. *Speaking Ill of the Dead: Jerks in Washington D.C. History*. Guilford, CT: Globe Pequot Press, 2011.

Johnson, L.F. *Famous Kentucky Tragedies and Trials*. Louisville, KY: Baldwin Law Book Co., 1916.

Kerr, Charles, ed. *History of Kentucky*. Vol. 4. Chicago, IL: American Historical Society, 1922.

Kleber, John E., ed. *The Kentucky Encyclopedia*. Lexington: University Press of Kentucky, 1992.

Klotter, James C. *Kentucky Justice, Southern Honor, and American Manhood*. Baton Rouge: Louisiana State University Press, 2003.

Lexington City Directory: 1838–39 and 1873–74. Located in Kentucky Room at Lexington Public Library.

Lexington, Fayette. *The Celebrated Case of Col. W.C.P. Breckinridge and Madeline Pollard*. Chicago, IL: Current Events Publishing Company, 1894.

Lexington Observer and Reporter. November 20, 1844.

Lucas, Marion B. *A History of Blacks in Kentucky*. Vol. 1. *From Slavery to Segregation, 1760–1891*. Frankfort: Kentucky Historical Society, 1992.

Maysville Evening Bulletin. "Terrible Tragedy." November 9, 1889.

McQueen, Keven. *Cassius M. Clay*. Nashville, TN: Turner Publishing Co., 2001.

———. *Offbeat Kentuckians*. Kuttawa, KY: McClanahan, 2001.

New York Times. "Breckinridge Is Hissed." February 2, 1895.

———. "Col. Breckinridge's Alibis." March 27, 1894.

———. "A Congressman in Trouble." August 13, 1893.

———. "Did Not Mean to Marry Her." March 18, 1894.

———. "Farnsworth Sends Challenge." January 1, 1902.

———. "Giving Evidence for Miss Pollard." March 10, 1894.

———. "The Last of Colonel Goodloe." November 11, 1889.

———. "Miss Pollard Disparaged." March 29, 1894.

———. "Miss Pollard Now Testifies." March 17, 1894.

———. "Shot Dead in His Tracks." November 17, 1887.

———. "Wants to Fight a Duel." December 28, 1901.

Ramage, James A. *Rebel Raider: The Life of John Hunt Morgan*. Lexington: University Press of Kentucky, 1995.

Raymond, M., Reverend. *God Goes to Murderer's Row*. Milwaukee, WI: Bruce Publishing Company, 1951.

Reed, William F. "One of a Kind Legendary Coach Adolph Rupp—Loved by Some, Loathed by Others—Turned Kentucky Basketball into a Dynasty." *Sports Illustrated*, April 17, 1996.

Report of the Vice Commission of Lexington, KY. 1915. Printed in Lexington. Located in Kentucky Room at Lexington Public Library.

Rhyne, J. Michael. "'Conduct…Inexcusable and Unjustifiable': Bound Children, Battered Freedwomen, and the Limits of Emancipation in Kentucky's Bluegrass Region." *Journal of Social History* (Winter 2008): 319–40.

Runyon, Randolph Paul. *Delia Webster and the Underground Railroad*. Lexington: University Press of Kentucky, 1999.

Sabine, Lorenzo. *Notes on Duels and Dueling*. Boston, MA: Crosby, Nichols, & Co., 1855.

Schmitz, Brian. "Add a Touch of Black to Kentucky's Blue." *Orlando Sentinel*, May 13, 1997.

Smith, Caroline Turner. *Caroline Augusta Sargent Turner*. Chatham, NJ: Diamond Pyramid Enterprises, 1995.

Smith, Gerald L. *Lexington, Kentucky*. Charleston, SC: Arcadia, 2002.

Tapp, Hambleton, and James C. Klotter. *Kentucky: Decades of Discord 1865–1900*. Frankfort: Kentucky Historical Society, 1977.

Thompson, Buddy. *Madam Belle Brezing*. Lexington, KY: Buggy Whip Press, 1983.

Townsend, William H. *Lincoln and the Bluegrass*. Lexington: University of Kentucky Press, 1955.

———. *The Most Orderly of Disorderly Houses*. Lexington, KY: privately printed, 1966.

Various. *Born in Slavery: Slave Narratives from the Federal Writers' Project, 1936–1938*. On file at the Library of Congress. http://memory.loc.gov/ammem/snhtml/snhome.html.

Warren, Robert Penn. *All The King's Men*. New York: Harcourt, 2001.

Warsaw Daily Times. "In His Own Behalf." March 30, 1894.

———. "The Tattler." July 31, 1897.

Wayne County Democrat. "Owen's a Winner." September 19, 1894.

Weekly Herald Baltimore. "Breckinridge Confident." May 11, 1894.

Weeks, Jeffrey. "The Body and Sexuality." In Hall, Stuart et al., eds. *Modernity: An Introduction to Modern Societies*. Oxford: Open University, 1996, 363–94.

Wilson, Douglas L. *Honor's Voice: The Transformation of Abraham Lincoln*. New York: Vintage, 1999.

Wright, George C. *A History of Blacks in Kentucky*. Vol. 2. *In Pursuit of Equality, 1890–1980*. Frankfort: Kentucky Historical Society, 1992.

———. *Racial Violence in Kentucky, 1865–1940*. Baton Rouge: Louisiana State University Press, 1990.

Wright, John D. *Lexington: Heart of the Bluegrass*. Lexington, KY: Lexington–Fayette County Historic Commission, 1982.

Yandell, Lunsford P. *Memoir of Dr. Benjamin W. Dudley*. Louisville, KY: J.P. Morton, 1870.

ABOUT THE AUTHOR

Fiona Young-Brown is a freelance writer and editor. Originally from England, she spent several years living in Japan before moving to Kentucky ten years ago. With an academic background in American history and women's studies, as well as a personal love of genealogy, she soon developed a keen interest in Lexington's more colorful characters. Her work has appeared in a number of magazines, including *Kentucky Monthly* and *American Cowboy*. This is her second book about the history of Lexington.

Visit us at

www.historypress.net